MIND YOUR OWN BUSINESS

www.ingramcontent.com/pod-product-compliance
Lightning Source LLC
Chambersburg PA
CBHW031855200326
41597CB00012B/418

MIND YOUR OWN
BUSINESS

The Small Business Owner's Relentless
Pursuit of Multigenerational Wealth

PAUL L. MARRELLA

J.D., CFP®

LIONCREST
PUBLISHING

MIND YOUR OWN BUSINESS
The Small Business Owner's Relentless Pursuit
of Multigenerational Wealth

ISBN   978-1-5445-0576-3 *Paperback*
       978-1-5445-0575-6 *Ebook*

To Dad:

Growing up, you demanded a lot of us kids. "Good enough" never really was. You had a unique ability to teach us life's lessons verbally, by example, and through sports, all so that we could be the best we could be. The value of hard work, discipline, and resilience became part of who we are. These life lessons allowed all of us to succeed in our own individual way. You were relentless in making sure we had the grit to succeed. We probably don't say thank you often enough...every time you see this book on your shelf, consider it a tacit thank you from not only me, but all four of us kids.

CONTENTS

INTRODUCTION

A hard thing about business is minding your own.

—UNKNOWN

I come from a family of competitors. Whether it's a game of Monopoly on Thanksgiving or early mornings on the basketball court, we're bonded not just by blood, but by the drive to win.

From the time we could walk, my brother and I were out on the field or the court playing whatever sport we could: basketball, football, baseball, or even games that we invented ourselves; you name it. We'd stay out sunup to sundown, playing until our mother rang the bell for us to come home. We didn't know theater and we weren't big readers, but boy, did we love playing any kind of ball.

Over the years, the more I've thought about it, the more I've realized that everything I know about life, I learned from sports.

Growing up, our coaches instilled in us the pursuit of excellence. Their methods were simple—they made sure we worked harder than everyone else, and they drilled into us the importance of not only mastering the fundamentals, but building an athlete's mindset. We learned to develop a quiet confidence, a belief that we could compete against anyone and persevere through anything. Most importantly, my coaches believed in teaching us not only how to win—but how to *lose*.

When you understand losing, the sensation of pain and disappointment never leaves you. To be a competitor, and to play to win, you must commit yourself wholeheartedly to avoiding a loss at all costs. You have to live with tough emotions. You have to be able to rebound from a setback and better yourself for the next battle. More than anything, you have to keep going. You can't quit. You can't abandon your purpose.

I believe that the strength to recover from loss requires, above all else, personal fortitude: the resolve to stay true to your fundamental beliefs, no matter what life throws at you.

As an adult, I looked back on my childhood of sports with

incredible gratitude. I wasn't facing a countdown clock or an opposing defense anymore, but my problems as a professional seemed just as high-stakes as a shot to beat the buzzer. Thanks to the years I'd spent honing my fortitude as an athlete, I was always able to tackle big problems with determination and see them through to the end.

When I became a financial planner, I was suddenly on the other side of the desk watching clients face the biggest problem of their lives: how to plan their retirement. I was now the coach, trying to instill the same principles I'd learned playing sports.

Make no mistake—planning a retirement is a mountainous task. Add on the ambition many of my clients have to pass down wealth through multiple generations, and they find themselves staring down a goal they have no idea how to accomplish. They don't even know where to start.

If you've faced the same problems and uncertainties, or if you're facing them right now, then you are the person for whom I wrote this book.

SUCCESS BEGINS WITH FUNDAMENTALS

As a budding athlete, I sweated through early morning practices nearly every single day. We always started with the same thing: drills. Our coaches would run us through the fundamentals of the movements we needed to master over and over. We practiced these drills so consistently that they took root in our instincts. We didn't know it at the time, but we were building life skills that meant more than almost anything we learned in school: that success is even more difficult without unwavering fundamentals and discipline.

As a wealth manager, this is where I start. If my clients don't understand and practice the fundamentals, then no amount of advice and planning will bring them satisfaction and security.

Please understand that finding success and financial independence is a marathon, not a sprint. You must wake up every single day and know inside and out the goals you want to achieve. You need to design a clear playbook with your endgame in your mind, with full color and intricate detail. No matter what that goal looks like, making it a reality takes the personal conviction to stay the course.

Put more simply, you must first determine where you are today. Then determine where you want to go. Finally, you need someone to help you fill in the gaps and guide you along the way.

Like any sport, you can't win with a team of one; and when it comes to planning multigenerational wealth, you're playing a long game. People are living longer lives these days, and the ten- or twenty-year retirement of your parents' generation has become a thirty- or even forty-year stretch. That's a long playing field, and you'll need enough money to get you all the way to the end. Additionally, you'll face considerable obstacles—like inflation, for instance, which is no friend to a four-decade retirement. Planning your retirement is possibly the biggest problem you'll face at this point in your life. There is no boilerplate template to solve it.

That's my aim with this book. You will see what a vivid picture of multigenerational wealth looks like and how you build the mindset necessary to achieve it.

By the time you're done reading this playbook, you'll know the drills you need to practice to master the fundamentals. You will know the enemies you face and how you should approach them. You will also know how to assemble your team of coaches, who will help you get all the way down the field with the ball.

You'll gain a stronger grasp of the questions you need to ask yourself and your professional advisors in order to reach your goals, and you'll finish with a better understanding of how to approach your planning and the various facets of multigenerational wealth that need to be addressed.

Even more importantly, you will feel more confident that you can make smart decisions for yourself and your family and that there are solutions within your grasp. Confidence typically translates into better decisions, and better decisions result in better outcomes.

THE GOOSE, THE GOLD, AND YOU

A friend of mine who's been very successful in business once admitted to me, "Every day, I wake up and go to work out of nothing more than fear." His fear was not being able to take care of his family or not being able to maintain his family's lifestyle.

At first, his comment seemed unusual. *Why would he be scared?* I wondered.

Then, I quickly realized that I felt the same way. I, too, felt the fear of failure. The same feeling is true for *most* people, and especially so for entrepreneurs. When you own a business, it's all on you—the successes, the disappointments, the possibility of multigenerational wealth, and the potential for crushing loss. On a fundamental level, your goals for your business are simple. You want to provide for your family. You want to have the money to feed, clothe, and shelter them. You want to pay for their education and spend quality time with them on a vacation every once in a while. The possibility that your business might *not* do well enough to provide for those goals—the fear of failure—is understandably a source of pressure.

Here's the bottom line: the stress you're feeling is perfectly normal. In all honesty, this fear of failure is probably responsible in no small way for your success.

But Paul, you're thinking, *I don't want to go to work afraid every day.*

Understood. Let's try thinking about your business differently. For you, it's more than just a company; it's your livelihood. Your business is your own personal goose that lays golden eggs—figuratively, of course, like the fairytale creature. You've nurtured your goose over the years, in good times and bad. As it has grown and will continue to grow, it's laid eggs of different sizes and quantities. It's up to you to watch over your goose and ensure that it stays healthy, all the while realizing that nothing in the future is certain.

Your goose might fall ill or the goose might grow old, resulting in fewer eggs. Your business may hit a rough patch, the market may shift, trends might change. There may come a time when you, the caretaker of the goose—the person whose heart and soul is ingrained in your company—get sick or become incapacitated. What then? Who will care for your business?

The truth is that the care and management of your business is encompassed in all the different facets of wealth management planning.

Yes, wealth is about your company, but it's about taking care of yourself and your family as well. Without you, who will be left to keep things going? Many of our clients admit they've never thought about their business and its care in this way, but it's been helpful for them to understand how many contingencies they need to plan for.

Business owners face three main financial concerns.

1. The first involves taking care of the goose, **making sure your company stays healthy,** so it will continue to lay golden eggs.
2. The second is **allocating those eggs wisely so both you and your business continue to thrive,** increasing the probability you'll be able to weather the inevitable rough patches inherent in our economy.
3. The third is **taking care of yourself** so you're able to properly care for the first two concerns.

These three elements are intertwined, and any complete financial plan for multigenerational wealth must take all three into account. For most business owners, their biggest asset is the income generated from their business—yet they often don't think of it that way.

FIND OUT WHAT YOU DON'T KNOW

Author Roy H. Williams once wrote, "A smart man makes a mistake, learns from it, and never makes that mistake again. But a wise man finds a smart man and learns from him how to avoid the mistake altogether."

This quote has been a guide for me in everything I've accomplished. It's so strongly applicable to the planning of family wealth, too; when setting off on the journey to provide for generations in the future, the first step should be to find an expert to guide you.

If you polled one hundred business-owner families and one hundred non-business-owner families, you'd find that many of them worry about the same things: running out of money during retirement, leaving a lasting legacy, and not being a burden on their kids. Another often-overlooked concern we hear is the care of a "nonfinancial" spouse in case the "financial" spouse passes away. Persistent worries like these often shape retirement planning.

What's most important is to be aware of your own situation and needs, while being able to make objective, sound long-term financial decisions. That's why defining your personal focus is so critical.

Having the right mindset in wealth planning is difficult to define. The good news is that you will immediately recognize it when you see it. Few people understand the true complexity of managing wealth. One way is to educate yourself and learn from your own mistakes. Another approach is to learn from the mistakes of others. This will teach you how to prevent problems, both foreseeable and unforeseeable, before they happen. A third approach is to find someone with the expertise and experience to handle the ongoing issues vital for sound multigenerational wealth planning. A great trick is to remember that managing your wealth is like managing your business. So, ask yourself: *how would I handle similar decision-making within my business?* This book will help you answer that question.

To achieve multigenerational wealth, you have to make a lifetime of smart, long-term financial decisions. This involves considerably more than just investment decisions. You need to manage your taxes, transfer your wealth efficiently, and protect your assets from being unjustly taken.

It's a huge task, and it will require the utmost in fortitude.

THE COACH AND THE CADDY

Unlike most sports, golf allows a coach on the field of play, called a caddy. The caddy's job is to assist the player in all facets of the game, and the relationship requires the player's absolute confidence.

In the 2008 US Open, Tiger Woods was 101 yards away from the flag on the seventy-second and final hole, trailing by one stroke and buried in deep grass. He needed to put the ball in the hole in two shots—what golfers call "up and down."

Tiger's original thought was to hit a fifty-six-degree sand wedge. Then his caddy, Steve Williams, intervened and suggested he hit a sixty-degree wedge instead. With all his knowledge and skill, the caddy knew Tiger would have to swing harder to produce more backspin, and thus hope to keep the ball from bouncing and running away from the hole. Tiger asked his caddy to think it through, then took his recommendation. Tiger's shot came to rest fifteen feet from the hole, leaving him a putt to tie the championship and force an eighteen-hole playoff.[1]

Tiger was forced to make that last downhill putt on bumpy greens trampled by the other seventy players earlier that day. They both agreed Tiger should aim just outside the right edge of the hole, yet the putt had to be struck perfectly. As you probably guessed, he sank the putt and tied the tournament, placing him in an eighteen-hole playoff that Monday. He went on the next day to win the championship.

---

1 Bob Harig, ESPN Senior Writer, June 14, 2009, http://www.espn.com/golf/usopeno9/columns/story?columnist=harig_bob&id=4256164

THE CADDY'S ROLE

Why do I bring up the role of the caddy in a book on finance? Consider the British Open, which takes place in the UK each year. Playing and weather conditions in the UK tend to differ drastically from those in the US during the summer months. To prepare for this event, players often arrive a week ahead of the competition to begin practicing in these foreign conditions. While players reacquaint themselves, caddies walk the course, marking it and taking notes long before the tournament begins. Their job is to know every step, every terrain change of every hole. They are thinking through possible scenarios and challenges. They're making notes on the course and writing numbers in the yardage books. The caddy's job is to be prepared to adapt to unexpected situations on the fly. They do not know when or where they will be needed, but they must always be prepared before, during, and even after play. In essence, they are the player's most trusted advisor.

Now consider the role of your professional advisors—your attorney, your accountant, your financial advisor. Their job is to know everything about you, your family, and your financial world; to chart out the course; and to be able to adapt when the situation calls for it. They must be keenly familiar with your personal situation and goals in great detail. You never know when you will need them to lend advice, but they must make sure everyone is prepared to act when called upon. They help by figuring out your strategy and knowing everything they can about the obstacles before they may arise. Wealth managers coordinate the planning among your various professionals, much like a financial caddy.

As famous UCLA men's basketball coach John Wooden said, "Whatever you do in life, surround yourself with smart people who'll argue with you."

WINNING ON THE BACK NINE ON SUNDAY

Each part of this book focuses on one of the key aspects of multigenerational wealth planning:

1. In the first part, you'll envision your personal playbook, discovering clarity about who you are and what you want to accomplish.
2. In the second, you'll come up with a game plan, understanding the major obstacles you need to be thinking about as you plan for the future, and execute on that plan.
3. In the third, you'll find your financial caddy to maintain the ongoing planning necessary to help accomplish goals and avoid major problems.

This book will show you how to prepare—just like being ready to compete on Sunday in a major golf tournament—

by getting into the mindset required for financial success. You'll find each concept in these pages laid out in simple, easy-to-understand terms. After all, clarity is the key to planning for the future—the better your vision and understanding, the better your chance of achieving your goals.

With every piece of advice offered in these pages, my hope is that you're able to gain more valuable insight, affording you more confidence and direction on your journey to multigenerational wealth.

All the best!

PART ONE

ONLY YOU CAN

PLAN YOUR

PLAYBOOK

In every aspect of your life, have a game plan, and then do your best to achieve it.

—ALAN KULWICKI

Although a wealth manager may fulfill the metaphorical role of a financial caddy, the complete landscape of wealth management is more analogous to a team sport. At the planning outset, you are the owner, general manager, and star player of your team—and that means being aware of your strengths and weaknesses. Ultimately *you* must create the vision as to what you want the future to look like. Your game plan must be structured to keep you in the playoffs each and every year; you may not win the championship every year, but you will need to manage through good times and bad. As you consider your game plan for financial success and multigenerational wealth, you now have to consider not only this season, but the many seasons to come.

To design your personal playbook, you need to know where you are today and where you want to go. Although it sounds simple, being objective and reasonable is sometimes difficult when doing it yourself. For many business owners, sometimes you have to start by looking backward—to remember who you are and where you came from.

Creating, growing, and running a business is stressful. In

the startup phase, you jump in, work hard to get off the ground, and then hope for business to come rolling in. In the growth phase, your company takes off and you can't seem to keep up with the demand. With each following phase, there are more decisions to make, and the obstacles you face become more complicated.

When I was going through these phases myself, I wanted to perform well and go the extra mile. I wanted to create relationships. I wanted to be someone people would rely on. But balancing business and family was difficult, each with its own emotional roller coaster that got more hectic when times were difficult.

The question is *why*: *why* do we put ourselves through so much stress and struggle just to make a business work?

The answer, of course, is that we want to provide for ourselves and our families. There's also a joy and excitement that comes with taking on the responsibility of being your own boss. The rewards, the feeling of accomplishment, are irreplaceable.

At some point, however, the *why* shifts. It may be that your determination to succeed becomes deeper, or you want to see your business's value maximized long term. It may be that when you started out, you only needed to provide for yourself, but now you have a spouse, children, and perhaps even grandchildren to provide for. You have their futures to think about. You may be realizing that your retirement is approaching more quickly than you imagined. Whatever the reason, the drive behind your conviction to press on is likely a mixture of habit, perseverance, and fear.

So, take a look back. Why did you start your business? What made you choose the work you do? If you started your business to make money, did you have a larger goal in mind as well, or has that shifted over time? Your personal, family, and financial values are unique. Interestingly, nearly all business owners want to incorporate these values into their planning and pass them on to the next generations.

Now, let's look to the future. Where do you want to take your business in the years to come? Do you want to grow your business so you can sell it and invest or live off the proceeds? Or do you want your business to last forever and be passed down to generations that follow? Will you establish a family legacy through a foundation?

Beyond your business, what do you want your family's lifestyle to look like, and how much will it cost? Where will you live? Will you have more than one home? Remember, you're calling the shots, but the specific outcomes you desire will require different types of planning and expertise.

Regardless, only you can paint the picture of what you want to accomplish. The goals, desires, and dreams must be yours, otherwise the drive to succeed at planning will inevitably fade.

Multigenerational wealth planning starts with a complicated math problem. First, you need to understand there is a cost to everything you want to do, starting with your remaining work years, then your retirement, and ultimately your wealth transfer. Many people in their working years, for instance, don't notice costs like travel and entertainment; they're just focused on saving enough to afford retirement. But an awareness of these costs is critically important.

Costs need to be adjusted for inflation, because costs tend to rise over time. Food, vacations, and automobiles will most likely cost more down the road. Fortunately for the mathematically challenged, there is software to help with this planning. Whatever the case, your goals are unique to you and there are calculable costs for everything you want to do.

Also worth noting is that wealth is relative. To some people, $10 million is more money than they can spend in three lifetimes, while to others it's the price of their yacht. For most, creating multigenerational wealth requires larger sums of money than they expect. Few business owners realize just how much money they regularly spend and how much they will need to be financially independent. If you underestimate your annual lifestyle costs after retirement—or simply fail to plan—you may be in for a surprise. Will you save and invest adequately for retirement...or will you still be tied to your business, coaxing your goose to lay more and more eggs in your (and perhaps the goose's) golden years?

Once you know what you want to achieve with those golden eggs, you can continue to plan ahead. Eventually—whether due to retirement, disability, or death—the goose stops laying those precious golden eggs, and then you'll need to fall back on your savings to fund your lifestyle. The question to ask yourself before you get to that point is: *how much risk am I willing to take?* You've got to think about the golden eggs while you're still working. Will you risk keeping all of your wealth in your business, or will you increase your personal wealth outside the business? The most conservative advice is to diversify your business holdings into personal wealth. Then, if the goose dies or lays fewer eggs, you don't lose everything. We'll look at this strategy, and others, in the chapters to come.

Every play in this playbook is up to you and those you entrust to assist. Your team will help you execute your game plan. Your vision is necessary to determine the outcome, but once your vision is well defined, you can sit back and trust your team to execute.

Will you win or will you lose? The chapters that follow will show you the obstacles you have to face and help you design a strategy that plays to your strengths. It's time to plan for games ahead. Get your Xs and Os ready, and let's get started.

CHAPTER ONE

SEEING YOUR OBSTACLES

The game plan might be different based on the opponent, but the approach is the same.

—ANDRE WARD

If you, like so many business owners, don't have a plan for financial success, you may feel like you are teeing off, hitting your ball into the bright blue sky, with no idea where the green is—or what hazards may lie between you and the hole itself.

Think back to your first year, your first day, your first minute at work. What was it like? In those first few years, you were probably winging it for just about every task you were given. Time floated by as you worked long hours, trying to find time to hang out with friends after hours and have some fun. There would be plenty of time later to worry about the big decisions.

One day, you wake up and it's twenty years later. Your life and career have surpassed your wildest expectations. Perhaps somewhere in there you got married and had children. Life and success seem to have happened overnight. But, you wonder, where did all this responsibility come from? How did your business get to this size? Most of all, what should you do now?

Have you already waited too long to plan?

THE "INEVITABLES"

The longer you're in business, the more difficult your decisions become. You must deal with ever-changing complications, what I sometimes call "inevitables," both expected and unexpected. Living your life without your business is inevitable, so you may as well start planning now for your business (the goose) to function without you.

Multigenerational wealth planning has similar inevitables. The earlier you understand the obstacles you face, the better. The three biggest hurdles to your success are fear, change, and the unforeseeable.

FEAR

While fear of failure is a significant part of owning a business, the fear of managing money, keeping up on tax laws, and planning for retirement successfully can be just as consuming. Just as intimidating. And just as crippling to your success.

There are two kinds of people in the world: those who love finance, and those who avoid it at all costs. "Financial people" more often embrace the responsibilities related to wealth management. Nonetheless, they seldom have time to become highly skilled, let alone oversee it successfully. Those who prefer to avoid dealing with finances often make the worst possible decision in multigenerational planning: they do nothing at all. Conversations about money, inflation, retirement income planning, and investing in the capital markets cause these people to shut down. When this happens, it's often because of an underlying fear.

As Nelson Mandela said, "I learned that courage was not the absence of fear, but the triumph over it. The brave man is not he who does not feel afraid, but he who conquers that fear." As you learn to take control of your financial future, it is unreasonable to expect that you will never feel fear. Overcoming that fear by facing it head-on should help you create a winning plan.

CHANGE

Fear can be compounded by the ever-changing economy and constantly evolving rules associated with running a business. The expertise needed to accomplish business goals takes considerable knowledge and continuing education. For those who aren't financially minded, not keeping up with these changes can create a huge knowledge gap between what they *should* know about wealth management and what they think they know.

You and your business will inevitably face both good economies and bad, so you need to prepare for both. Financial behaviors tend to worsen when the economy is faltering. These negative changes increase the likelihood of making poor financial decisions for yourself and your business. Little things like keeping money in reserve usually mean you don't "overspend" in good times. They also increase your chances of weathering those bad times. Another "boom" economy risk is investing in speculative investments that seem too good to be true.

As the world changes—and it inevitably will—recognizing the effects of those changes on your wealth and your planning will be one of the best safeguards against potential missteps.

THE UNFORESEEABLE

The old saying is true: "Failing to plan is planning to fail." When people don't have a general plan in place to encompass the unforeseeable—the things you can't create a specific plan for—they fail to consider the potential disaster when something inevitably goes wrong.

On May 22, 2014, our city had a major hailstorm. Hailstorms in our area are rare, and the weather channels reported that the one coming was "possible," but no one expected it to happen. The hail, which ranged in size from golf balls to tennis balls, wrecked everything in its path: cars, landscaping, even buildings. Nothing was spared.

Rarely do multiple people suffer from the same unforeseeable event on such a large scale as we experienced with this hailstorm. Never had so many of my clients faced the same losses from the same problem on the same day. And it quickly became evident that there was a large gap between what different insurance companies were willing to pay for my clients' claims. The clients who had taken the time to get proper coverage and were willing to pay for more than "no-frills" insurance faced fewer surprises. While they had higher payments along the way, these clients had considered the real long-term cost savings and confidence. They knew that, in a disaster, those costs would pay for themselves over and over. And they understood what it takes to plan for the unforeseeables.

This is just one example of the unforeseeables we need to prepare for. When your primary responsibility is caring for the goose, will you recognize potential problems? More important, will you be prepared for any circumstance, good or bad? Protecting yourself and your business from the unexpected requires additional planning expertise. Doing so can be the difference between feeling the relief of knowing you planned for the unexpected, and experiencing the panic that ensues when you know you haven't.

GET AHEAD OF THE GAME

Business owners must plan for the good, the bad, and the ugly, but few do. Being able to solve problems is a valuable skill. What's even more valuable is the experience to visualize what might go wrong and properly plan before potential problems arise. These planning skills are vital to protecting the goose and your family. This planning takes time and energy, which many business owners fear will disrupt their business, which may be true. Equally true is that if a problem arises for which you are unprepared, your business and your family may be irreparably affected. An ounce of prevention may be worth a pound of cure.

LEARNING TO BE SMART

If you were a billionaire—and who knows, maybe you are—would you handle all the aspects of your affairs:

your business ventures, real estate, taxes, etc.? More likely than not, you'd hire the best attorneys, accountants, and management teams to maximize the value of both your time and your business interests. You'd have an entire board of skilled men and women all trying to make informed, smart decisions. The only difference is that for the billionaire, money is no object and top talent typically costs more to employ.

A business associate of mine once said, "When I call a lawyer, I want the top partner whose name is on the door. I realize his/her hourly rate is usually three times his underling's, but I typically get the answer before I get off the phone and don't have to pay someone to research the answer. It saves both of us time and money."

Kind of smart, isn't it?

How do you handle your vital and complicated ventures in your business? When you have highly technical problems, don't you engage your best (usually highest-paid) employees for solutions?

Many business owners wrestle with paying someone else to handle their wealth management. We all want to believe we can make time to learn everything we need to be successful and profitable, but for most of us, that's just not going to happen.

I come from a hard-working, disciplined, and somewhat proud family. We never hired anyone to do the work around our house that we could do ourselves, because in our minds that meant we were forgetting where we came from.

Years later—after I'd redefined my career goals, started my own family, and returned home to reinvent the family business—I tried to balance all the various aspects of my life, but I wasn't doing a great job.

One Friday when I got home from work, took off my necktie, and prepared to spend the next hour mowing the lawn, my wife said, "Why don't you pay someone to take care of the grass?"

My response was, "Over my dead body! I will *never* pay someone to do that for me." That's just not how I was raised.

But then she said something that made me think. "Paul, you already work so hard. The hour you spend cutting the grass is an hour you're not spending with the kids."

The next week, I had hired someone to cut the lawn. It made sense to have someone else handle one of the things I didn't need to do, so I could focus on the people who mattered most. True, finding the right landscaper is far less challenging than finding the right person to share your most sacred personal and financial information and goals with—but the need to outsource services is the same as in any other aspect of business and life.

Let's think about multigenerational wealth planning in terms of a business owner's way of thinking.

You wake up in the middle of the night and you've dreamt up a bright idea for a new product, which we will call the "Widget." You immediately grab a piece of paper and begin jotting down everything you can think of for the product, including what it will look like, how it can be used, and how it can be produced ("your vision").

Over the next few weeks you expand upon your vision, testing the viability and potential profitability of the Widget. Then you consider the Widget's design and whether it is economically feasible, both of which require specific expertise. Next, you need to consider potential design flaws and consider what can go wrong while the product is being used. Hopefully, you will even be able to get a patent for your new invention. Again, additional levels of expertise are required.

When you think of what can go wrong, you need to consider what types of potential product liability there are, which is probably beyond your expertise. Purchasing the necessary liability insurance would probably make sense as well.

What if something happens to you, and you've never shared your vision with anyone on your team? The possibility exists that the Widget's secrets vanish into thin air because they were not documented. Again, these are other areas of expertise to accomplish your goals. As time goes on, you also want to consider various improvements in both the Widget's design and manufacture. Planning your financial future is really no different. Only you can come up with the dream of what you want it to look like ("your vision"). For most of our clients, the importance of money is to allow them to do what they want to do, when they want to do it and where they want to do it.

If you want a winter or summer home, there is a cost for that. If you want to drive luxury cars or own an expensive boat, there is a cost for that. Just like the Widget, you need to make sure this is affordable. You need to create a plan to produce the necessary income for your retirement, and it has to be economically viable. Just like manufacturing the Widget, you need to design your retirement plan to match your goals, which requires a specific expertise. The vision *is* in your head; it's just a matter of documenting it, just like the Widget. Sometimes you need the right questions asked so you can crystallize them into actionable thoughts.

What about things that could go wrong? You could get sick, need long-term care, or suffer from a terrible accident. What if something unforeseeable happens? You need to protect yourself from catastrophic events, which requires additional expertise. Like liability insurance, there are ways to protect yourself from some of these potential problems.

Who's going to make decisions for you if you become old or infirm? Again, you need specific planning from someone experienced in these areas.

I don't care whether you have $100 million in the bank or own a business generating $5 million a year—you have to take care of the tough stuff. There may be risks you can't even foresee that have extremely low probability but immensely large consequences.

Here's the key: all aspects of life are far more complicated than they used to be. You can really only be an expert in one field. Whether you're building the Widget or planning your multigenerational wealth, you have to surround yourself with capable, trustworthy experts. A team of professional advisors (attorneys and accountants, along with insurance and financial advisors) can help you see all sides of a decision so you make the wisest choice possible. With knowledgeable advisors on your side (just like your company's board), you are far more likely to make smart long-term decisions. Incidentally, you will have more time and energy to focus on your business *and* your family.

If you are struggling to overcome this bias, ask yourself what your family's future well-being is worth. What's the cost of making a mistake? Is it worth getting the advice that could be the difference between financial struggle and financial independence?

You might also find interesting how many securities professionals hire advisors themselves. I have a lot of dealings with home office personnel, discussing technology and wealth management issues. More often than not, they say, "When I talk with my advisor..."

I always ask, "Why would you have an advisor when you have a securities license yourself?"

Their response is inevitably, "I just don't have the time or expertise and don't trust myself to do it right."

When you get to the point where you realize you need help strategizing financially, it's time to find someone who can help you diagram the golf course, just like the PGA tour players do. Only when you know what to expect can you plan to play for par. Chapter 2 will help you consider how you can avoid water hazards, sand traps, and other bunkers so you can play through with confidence.

CHAPTER TWO

CONFIDENT DECISIONS

Whatever course you decide upon, there is always someone to tell you that you are wrong...To map out a course of action and follow it to an end requires courage.

—RALPH WALDO EMERSON

When I was a lawyer, my firm represented a gentleman selling his business to a large multinational company. The first day of negotiations lasted fourteen hours and covered all types of business matters, from human resources to sales. As the partner in charge advised the business owner on each detail, he brought each issue down to the most basic decision point—almost oversimplifying it to make the issue as clear as possible. You would be amazed to see how quickly our client was able to make decisive and confident decisions. Like a coach simplifying an entire game plan into Xs and Os, my boss was handing out straightforward plays to his starting quarterback. This was my first entrée into "a wise man teaching a smart man."

CHOOSE CONFIDENTLY

The quest for multigenerational wealth is all about what's important to you. Not only must you earn the money, but then you must save it, manage it, protect it, and ultimately decide if and how you will pass it on. There are countless difficult decisions to be made, and your personal situation will change. As your wealth increases, each planning choice gets more complicated. As complexity increases, knowledge and experience become more critical—but so does the potential lack of confidence.

Only you can decide what you want to accomplish, but you need to document it and be able to objectively evaluate where you currently stand and where you want to go. These conversations allow you to home in and specifically identify what you want to do—with a laser focus that will drive all of your decision-making processes, typically resulting in more confident choices.

Confidence is key. This is where the best advisors—

whether legal, accounting, or financial, coach or caddy—separate themselves. The best thing you can do is simplify each and every issue down to a level you (and those closest to you) can understand, into terms everyone is familiar with. You also need to understand both the pros and cons of each issue. If you don't fully comprehend the questions before you, you're far more likely to second-guess yourself, either now or in the future. Be sure to have all the information you need, in terms that are comfortable and clear to you.

Confident decisions, based on the most reliable information available to you at the time, are usually the best decisions. Your gut will give you a strong indication of how confident you truly are in the decision you're about to make. As you approach each situation, remember that sometimes good decisions lead to bad outcomes and, more dangerously, bad decisions can lead to good outcomes. When making a decision, do so with the conviction you made the right one for you and your family. You'll be more likely to stick with it, even if the immediate outcome is not favorable. Getting better at making confident decisions will serve you well. As General George S. Patton said, "When you have collected all the facts and fears and made your decision, turn off all your fears and go ahead!"

"SOUNDS SIMPLE ENOUGH"

Business owners face many challenges. You enter the office each day with your list of meetings and what you want to accomplish. Rarely, however, does your day flow the way you had planned. You simply have too many responsibilities. If you don't have different departments to handle various tasks, you become a talented, extremely busy jack-of-all-trades. If something catches fire, you put it out. But because you only have so much time and energy, you likely neglect other aspects of your life or business, including personal finance. While you're at work, you're taking care of the goose. When you get home, you're tired. You don't feel like working on anything else. Everyone knows it needs to be done; they just don't know where to start. You put financial planning off today, then tomorrow, then the next day, and before you know it you're fifty-five and it's still not started. You've gotten stuck in the habit of inaction.

Why? First, you may not understand all the ins and outs of what goes into planning, so you put it aside. Second, finance isn't your favorite way to spend your leisure time. Third, you don't know where to begin or find help.

As Meister Eckhart so perfectly put it, "The price of inaction is far greater than the cost of making a mistake." Preparing for multigenerational wealth requires a never-ending, almost guerilla-like ongoing quest to save, invest, and plan your finances. For busy business owners, planning often takes a back seat to their day-to-day activities.

Too many people simply don't plan. They might pick up this book, read through it, and think they don't need it because their finances seem under control; they've talked to someone and already thought about certain aspects. They have a general idea of what they want retirement to look like—to be comfortable and not worry about money. What else is there? Well, likely much more than you realize.

When you began learning math as a child, your teachers introduced addition and subtraction before they taught you algebra. They taught you a foundation. Knowledge is power, and it creates confidence, which promotes good financial decision making. Before you can make confident choices regarding wealth management, you must build a solid financial foundation. That foundation is based on asking yourself the hard questions and looking at your situation objectively.

ASK YOURSELF THE HARD QUESTIONS

KEY QUESTION #1: WHAT'S IMPORTANT TO YOU ABOUT MONEY?

While people have different opinions about money, when asked *why* it's important to them, many simply answer,

"It allows me to live comfortably." It allows them to do what they want, when and where they want to do it. This is what we call financial independence. While this is one of the first stages of wealth, it doesn't account for multi-generational wealth.

Taking care of yourself and your family requires long-range planning so you can maximize the use of your money during and after your lifetime. You need to prioritize what's important to you about money, whether that's improving your children's retirement or providing for your grandkids' educations.

Money's importance may be philanthropic, allowing your wealth to benefit others as well. For example, Bill and Melinda Gates want to "help all people lead healthy, productive lives."[1] Obviously, that requires not only considerable thought, foresight, and planning, but also considerable wealth. That's the plan they designed to use their wealth to achieve something important according to their values.

Whatever your personal priority, a long-term vision is a vital component of multigenerational planning.

---

1   "Who We Are: Foundation Fact Sheet," Bill and Melinda Gates Foundation, https://www. gatesfoundation.org/Who-We-Are/General-Information/Foundation-Factsheet.

KEY QUESTION #2: WHAT DO YOU WANT YOUR MONEY TO DO FOR YOU?

Without knowing what you want your money to do for you, you'll be planning your course without a destination. Everything in this world has a price tag. Fancy cars and lavish vacations are easy to acquire—you just have to be able to pay for them. Having the necessary resources to fund your lifestyle many decades into the future may be harder.

Some people choose to push ahead without carefully considering how much money their goals will require. They may have millions of dollars saved, which would seem significant to most people. Often, however, they fail to consider the long-term cost of their lifestyle and spend those millions without a plan. Living beyond our means almost seems to be the rule, rather than the exception in our society. Thomas J. Stanley, author of *The Millionaire Next Door*, said, "Many people who live in expensive homes and drive luxury cars do not actually have much wealth...Many people who have a great deal of wealth do not even live in upscale neighborhoods."

Consider what multigenerational wealth means to you. Your answer will be different from anyone else's, because everyone defines wealth in their own way. Understand what you want to accomplish and the steps necessary to get there. Yes, you might be lucky enough to make it without a plan, but *with* a plan, you know exactly where you're headed. A goal without a plan is just a wish.

KEY QUESTION #3: HOW MUCH WILL YOU NEED?

Unfortunately, many retirees fail to even consider the question of how much money they will need to comfortably live the rest of their lives. If they do attempt to answer it, most underestimate their retirement needs.

Your answer to this question will depend on your answers to the first two questions. Maybe you want to buy a new car every three years. Do you want a Ferrari or a Chevy sedan? The amount you'll need in order to buy a new car every three years for the rest of your life varies depending on the kind of car you buy—but the overall cost can be planned for if you are objective about your goals. Retirement planning is just a math problem, and the numbers don't lie.

You may have looked over your investments and savings and decided you're in good shape. You believe that you've planned, have a goal, and know how much money you need. But have you covered all the bases? Over the years, people have come to me with all kinds of self-assessments, from simple calculations to complicated spreadsheets, but there is almost always some major factor missing, like a failure to consider inflation.

Let's look at a simplified scenario. Suppose you want to spend $120,000 per year ($10,000 per month) beginning at age sixty-five. You should plan to live to age one hundred, meaning you will need $4.2 million (thirty-five years × $120,000) without inflation. Adjusted for inflation, however, that $4.2 million becomes $7.26 million. You may be able to spend $120,000 the year you turn sixty-five, but once you account for the effects of 3 percent inflation each year, you will need $216,733 the year you turn eighty-five. When you turn ninety-five, you will need $291,271 in order to maintain the same lifestyle that only cost $120,000 thirty years earlier.

Few people measure the effects inflation will have on their retirement. And fewer and fewer business owners have pensions, meaning they must build their own cash flow structure. Social Security will supplement your income, but the wealthier you are, the less impactful it will be. Also, recognize the possibility exists that Social Security policy changes could take place in the future.

Are you looking at your present spending, extrapolating into the future, and still coming to the conclusion that you're covered? Managing your retirement income planning is vital to your multigenerational wealth planning. It's difficult to plan for successive generations if you underestimate what you need for yourself.

KEY QUESTION #4: ONCE YOU KNOW HOW MUCH YOU NEED, DO YOU HAVE ENOUGH TO ACHIEVE YOUR GOALS?

Now that you know how much money you will need, do you have enough to make it last? Ideally, you will have "too much" money, but those with too much find themselves spending more, almost to the point of a shortfall.

If you find that you don't yet have enough, there are two "levers" you can pull: you can retire later, or you can spend less. The average American prefers the former to the latter.

Think back to the goose. How long can she continue laying golden eggs? How long do you want to wake up each day, worrying about taking care of the goose? The earlier you start planning, the more apt you are to understand what you want to do with the goose and when. You might begin the search for your successor so you can implement a slow transition out of work, which may extend your career and allow the goose to be more productive for you over a longer period of time. Or you might decide that it makes more sense to sell the goose, even if it is gut-wrenching to do so. Starting early gives you the time you need to make tough financial decisions with confidence and clarity.

If you understand your goals early on, each and every

decision may focus on that vision. Goals-based decision making allows you to select options based on what you want to achieve down the road, not what may make you "feel good" at the time. Anyone can be wealthy tomorrow, but the objective is to create the opportunities to succeed for the long term. Doing so allows you a better chance of maximizing your wealth. But remember, only you can paint the picture of what it is you want to achieve.

AN OBJECTIVE PARTNER

Have you ever wondered why business owners continue working long after they've earned more money than they can spend in ten lifetimes? It doesn't make sense, does it? Unless that business is *your* business. You may be able to happily spend your entire career focused on your business. It envelops you and becomes your passion; your business becomes part of who you are. But are you able to evaluate it objectively?

Business owners spend inordinate amounts of time making their business run efficiently and profitably. One of the most challenging aspects of achieving multi-generational wealth is people's inability to be objective about their situations. My dad always says, "It's difficult to be objective about two things: your children and your money." There's simply too much emotion about one's personal affairs, resulting in a cognitive bias.

Objectivity involves taking off the rose-colored glasses and moving past the belief that everything will work itself out if you just work hard and remain optimistic. One researcher wrote, "The basic gist behind this research is that what people think is true is often not true. We tend to think that how we see and view things reflects an objective reality, but this is often not the case."[2]

For example, some of my older clients often discuss downsizing their homes. Nine times out of ten, when I ask what they think their home is worth, they respond, "My neighbor just sold their home for $450,000, but ours is nicer because..." They may not see that, objectively, the houses are the same; they just like their house better because it is *theirs*. I also often ask clients for an idea of how much money they need to spend each year, so we can project the true cost of their lifestyle. Inevitably, nearly all say, "We don't spend that much money..." Meanwhile, they have three homes, six cars, and two boats. Spending is relative, but many struggle to think objectively about their financial situations because they do not want to face the potential "pain" of hearing they may need to make significant changes.

In order to take that first step toward seeing your situation for what it is, you must ask yourself the questions we just

---

2   Nathan A. Heflick, "Are We as Objective as We Think?" *Psychology Today*, May 1, 2012, https://www.psychologytoday.com/us/blog/the-big-questions/201205/are-we-objective-we-think.

discussed: *Where am I now, where do I want to be in the future, and how am I going to get there?* The latter question is the most demanding. It requires you to analyze your current wealth, then calculate how much you will need to accomplish your goals. The gap between the two numbers defines whether you have too much or too little. You also need to identify and plan for several aspects of wealth planning beyond investing. No small task.

Why is being fully aware and objective so difficult? As humans, we're just wired this way. We don't expect athletes to be objective in calling their own penalties; that's why we have referees. In the same way, you may need a referee to help you look at your plans with clear eyes. Because it is difficult to gain the necessary objectivity about one's own situation, a team of experts—whose job involves looking at your situation objectively—can help make these tough calls.

Where do you start? How do you find someone who can communicate in your language? Keep a few important points in mind as you begin to explore your options. The team of coaches you choose to work with will serve you best if they understand who you are, what your values are, and what you're trying to do. Your advisors should be individuals with whom you have good chemistry and can form a solid relationship, and who have the expertise, credentials, and experience to understand what you want to accomplish.

With a strong background and a solid relationship, your multigenerational wealth manager becomes not only your referee but your financial caddy. They will choose the right club for the best shot, helping you frame your goals around the purpose you've established and guiding you in fulfilling those goals. They're meant to be there for the long haul, walking alongside you, understanding the consequences when your goals change or shift. Your advisor will act as your advocate, giving you the knowledge and confidence to make sound financial decisions.

As you move into part 2 of this book, you'll learn about key elements of wealth management, the importance of having a strong wealth manager at your side, and how to create the best game plan for your team.

PART TWO

THE GAME PLAN: FUNDAMENTALS OF MULTIGENERATIONAL WEALTH

An expert is someone who has succeeded in making decisions and judgments simpler through knowing what to pay attention to and what to ignore.

—EDWARD DE BONO

You have a goose—your business—that lays golden eggs. How are you going to grow those eggs, to reinvest them into your business? If your goose lays seven eggs every day, you might put two of them back into your business to pay employees and cover the goose's healthcare. The tax man is certainly going to take a couple. You might allocate another one or two eggs toward personal spending money. The remaining eggs are what separate the wealthy from those who are not. The multigenerationally wealthy use these to add to their personal wealth, allowing them to prepare for the investable financial obstacles they will face down the road.

What if the goose starts laying nine eggs next year? While most Americans would spend the extra two eggs, there are those who will save those two eggs for a rainy day or invest them for future use. Those with clearly delineated goals tend to be relentless savers, since their goals are crystal clear. That's how wealth is built—and how it can increase over generations.

On the other hand, what if the goose starts laying only

five eggs, and then four? You still have to maintain the goose's health and pay your employees, but you also have to plan for yourself, because the goose may not be there forever. Your best option is to understand how the inevitable loss of the goose will impact you, and to always be prepared.

Planning is a fluid process. It changes because the world changes. Additionally, we all have unique financial situations with different personalities, family structures, and goals. We have different worldviews and appetites for risk. A one-size-fits-all financial plan might not help you achieve your ultimate goal of multigenerational wealth, and you are less likely to follow through on it. It certainly won't allow for changes to your goals or your personal and family circumstances.

You need a customized plan, one that is flexible enough to accommodate ongoing modifications. One that you constantly review and update along the way. But where can you find this kind of plan?

Well, if you were on the golf course, you would turn to your caddy. If you were on the football field, you would ask your coach, who has studied hundreds if not thousands of successful plays over the years. They know that some of the best advice can be gleaned from those who have found success before us.

In this case, let's look at what other financially successful business owners have learned. They focus on four key areas of wealth management:

1. **Making It and Keeping It.** Creating wealth, saving money, and avoiding paying more than your fair share in taxes.
2. **Enhancing It.** Managing wealth for a designated future purpose.
3. **Protecting It.** Avoiding the unjust seizure of property, whether by lawsuit or identity theft, and building walls of protection through insurance and legal documentation. This may also include protecting your family and their identities from unsavory people.
4. **Transferring It.** Planning for cost- and tax-efficient multigenerational wealth transfers and charitable giving. Planning may also include transferring wealth using strategies to protect assets from your beneficiaries' creditors and spouses.

In the coming chapters, you'll study the plays in each of these key areas and come up with a winning game plan for managing your multigenerational wealth.

CHAPTER THREE

MAKING IT AND KEEPING IT

Building a Healthy Financial Cycle

After two decades of personal finance reporting, I've heard every excuse in the book for not saving money. That said, none of them really hold up—at least over the long term.

—JEAN CHATZKY

In multigenerational wealth planning, making money is far more complex and important than simply turning a profit for your business. Profits are important, of course, but not nearly as important as what you do with them.

Your first business priority is to keep the goose laying eggs.

To keep your business competitive, you must continue reinvesting in it. You also need to take care of those who take care of you. As one of my clients says, "Take care of your people, and the money will follow."

What far too often gets lost is the need to reinvest in *yourself*. The old saying "Pay yourself first" is vitally important, yet it goes far beyond just putting money in the bank.

As a business owner, you are both the employer and employee. You should save personally, just as any other employee would save for themselves, but the challenge is finding the discipline to set aside a portion of your earnings—consider them dividends—to build personal wealth outside the business. This means using only a designated portion for bills or pleasure, without allowing your entire "paycheck" to slip through your fingers. Let's face it: the desire to spend is human nature.

You may also find it tempting to tie up all your funds in your business, but that can be disastrous. Just because your business is vibrant today doesn't mean it will be in the future. Think about what happened during the 2008–2009 recession: General Motors filed for bankruptcy, shareholders were wiped out, and the auto giant ended up being owned by the US government, along with the unions and all its creditors. Thousands of dealerships had to close, which drastically affected small business owners.[1] What if you had owned one of those dealerships? Your goose would have been cooked.

Most business owners simply should not take that risk. Setting money aside personally gives you the security of knowing that you, your family, and your business will have a better chance of surviving an unforeseeable mishap or disruption to your business.

TO SAVE IT, FIRST YOU MUST MAKE IT

It's easy to say, "Make money," but it can be difficult to actually do so when starting and growing a business. Of all the stages, Making It and Keeping It is the most challenging—yet it is also the most critical. Without taking the needed measures to make money and creating avenues to keep that money, you will have nothing to protect and nothing to grow.

These pointers can help you make the most of the Making It stage so you have something to save for later:

- Establish principles and goals. Try not to dwell on what you may have done wrong in the past. Instead, focus on your end goals so you can create the infra-

---

1   Chris Isidore, "GM Bankruptcy: End of an Era," CNN, June 2, 2009, https://money.cnn. com/2009/06/01/news/companies/gm_bankruptcy/.

structure and discipline to build wealth. You will need to relentlessly pursue your goals.

- Acknowledge that properly managing wealth will be difficult, requiring solutions to complex problems.
- Ensure your business is running properly. Few things are more important than the goose. Hiring the right employees, taking care of them, and taking care of your customers should be your primary focus. Isn't that what got you where you are today?
    - Have a good business plan in place. Today's economy moves fast, and so does your competition. For example, in 2018, Alphabet, Google's parent company, ranked twenty-second in total revenue on the Fortune 500 List.[2] Google is not even twenty-five years old.[3] What if they were your direct competitor? What if they someday compete with you? You will need to adapt and reinvent your business to survive.
    - Have someone to help ensure strong execution of that plan. Build a capable team around you whose objective is both caring for your goose and caring for your family. Enlist and enable employees and professional advisors to guide you through the decision-making processes. Have them challenge your ideas.

---

2   "Search Fortune 500," *Fortune*, http://fortune.com/fortune500/list/.

3   "From the Garage to the Googleplex," Google, https://www.google.com/about/our-story/.

- Focus your time. Making It is a function of your unique abilities, and the stage where you personally should spend the most time. Most business owners find that when they outsource the tasks of Keeping It, Enhancing It, and Protecting It, they increase the probability that these tasks are accomplished. It also allows them more time to care for the goose.
  - Our business coaches (yes, we have coaches too) say, "If someone can do it 75 percent as well as you, let them do it." Delegate time-consuming tasks and outsource what you can. Today's "gig economy" provides tremendous resources to leverage both your business and personal time.
- Maintain balance. All business owners want to maximize earnings in peak years, but they often struggle to maintain a healthy work-life balance. My dad always said, "They don't replay your kids' Little League games." Take care of yourself and your family so that you avoid burning out and have time to enjoy the life you have worked so hard to build. We'll talk about this in more detail later in the chapter.

SPEND IT (TIME) TO KEEP IT (MONEY)

Once you have nailed the Making It stage, you want to hang on to those hard-earned dollars. Saving doesn't have to be complicated, but it does require relentless discipline. It's easy to come up with a multitude of excuses to justify spending; it's a lot harder to recognize the consequences of not saving because they may not be realized for decades.

Business owners tend to face a few common financial hurdles. These include debt reduction, family education planning, and retirement. Retirement is often the greatest financial need, but it's also the furthest down the road, so most people put it off until last. Far too many people spend more time scheduling their vacations than they do managing their wealth.

Again, looking to those who have preceded us can add insight. Here are some commonalities among successful business owners who have accomplished their goals:

- *Always* have money set aside for a rainy day. Failure to do so can result in substantially increased costs (i.e., credit card interest).
- Use financial momentum to your advantage. "Financial momentum" is a term I use to describe that period in life when your money is working for you. You no longer need to finance home repairs, a new set of tires, or even a new car. In addition, your investments and savings are silently growing to achieve your long-term goals.
- Make and keep a budget that works for you, recognizing that budgeting can be done in different ways.

- Don't buy anything you don't have the money for, with the exception of larger purchases such as your home.
- Spend less than you earn, including paying bills, money spent on pleasure, and any everyday costs. Be a relentless saver. For example, when you receive an income tax refund, save or invest it. Don't use it for a vacation you really can't afford.
- Make smaller sacrifices now in order to do bigger things later in life.

Save religiously, spend wisely, and keep your eye on the prize. However you do it, be "Relentless" and make it a daily priority.

CREATE A TAX STRATEGY

A general principle in the US income tax code states that each dollar added to your wealth will be subject to income tax, whether now or in the future. No matter how much money you make and save, the "tax man" will get his share. Though taxes can sometimes be deferred, you can't be certain what the future of tax rates might hold. You should always consider your individual situation and continually monitor it with your tax advisor. Remember, it's not how much you make, but how much you keep.

Do you believe income taxes will be higher in the future?

How will that impact your situation? Some business owners prefer to pay more income tax today, rather than deferring it into the future. Your personal and business income tax planning should be an integral part of your long-term multigenerational wealth strategy. You and your tax advisor will have to make some educated decisions, because the best strategy for you and your business depends on your particular situation and objectives. Sound tax advice, especially looking to the future, may make a significant difference in your multigenerational planning.

You may also consider creating tax planning strategies within your business. While beyond the scope of this book, there are numerous retirement, disability, and life insurance plans available. Some options can reduce business risks to your family if there is a health event, while others can provide planning opportunities to positively impact your multigenerational wealth.

Coordinating your business and personal tax planning is vital, as is hiring the right CPA. Engaging the right professionals may safeguard that planning opportunities are not overlooked. Communication between the business owner and all their advisors (what we call "relationship management") has helped a multitude of business owners successfully plan with fewer surprises.

A HEALTHY BALANCE OF BUSINESS AND FAMILY

I often hear from clients with lofty business goals that they struggle to maintain a balance between family and work life. I know I've been as guilty of this as anyone. We tend to spend the majority of our time growing and nurturing the success of our businesses, which means less time is available for our spouses and children. The hope is that we earn more money, allowing more for us to "keep." But the real idea behind Keeping It is all-encompassing. Your health, your business, and your family are all integral to your success.

Unfortunately, many business owners discover this far too late. As they come to the point where their involvement in the company begins to slow down, they begin to shift their focus away from the business and back toward their personal life and family. They begin to realize how much they've missed, especially with their own children. The time they once devoted to their business is now their own again, and they want to dedicate it to their grandchildren in order to build relationships.

If you're at a point where you have the opportunity to make adjustments in your work-life balance—*before* your children are grown and out of the house—spend some time reevaluating what is important to you. What values do you want to uphold? What events and experiences do you want to make sure not to miss? Just as there has to be a balance among the money you spend, the money you reinvest into the business, and the money you save, there has to be a balance between the time you give to your business and the time you devote to your family. If you surround yourself with the right team and empower them to make decisions, your business will thrive and you will have time to spend on what's most important to you. Remember, the wealthiest man in the world cannot buy himself more time. Making It and Keeping It applies to every facet of life.

PUT YOUR PRINCIPLES INTO PRACTICE

To some, the ideas of being tax smart, spending less than you make, and setting aside money to save and invest might appear obvious. The reality is that they're simple enough concepts, but still difficult to carry out. Many business owners become accustomed to an extravagant lifestyle. They don't plan ahead for expenses like their children's education, then either borrow money or use their retirement accounts to pay for them, never adjusting their lifestyle.

This book encompasses a lifetime of human observations from various professional angles. You might be surprised how similar the mindset is among the multigenerationally wealthy, whether they are business owners or not. Continue to observe their commonalities. Find ways to incorporate their philosophies so that you can build on them and meld them with your own principles. With the foundations of Making It and Keeping It in place, you can begin to build toward the next stage of financial success: Enhancing It.

CHAPTER FOUR

ENHANCING IT

Investing Early and Wisely

Sometimes my mistake has been hesitancy about acting on the decisions I've made. When's the best time to invest? It's today, not tomorrow.

—CHARLES SCHWAB

One distinct advantage of growing up in the home of multigenerational wealth proponents is that those concepts are ingrained from a very early age. When I graduated from law school and began my first "real" job as an attorney, my annual salary was about $30,000. Only a few months into my career, my father called me and said, "I need a check for $2,000."

Surprised, I replied, "For what?"

"For your IRA contribution," he responded. (At the time, $2,000 was the annual IRA limit.)

At twenty-four years of age, I thought I knew better than he did. "Dad, I'm a lawyer now. I'm going to make a lot of money, so I can worry about saving later."

"Okay," he said, "just get me a check tomorrow." So I did.

January second of the next year, he called me again. "Where's your check for $2,000?" he asked.

A similar discussion ensued, and then my check was in the mail. As I'm sure you've guessed, the same thing transpired the next January. And the next. The value of his advice didn't hit me right away. When I opened my IRA statement a few years later, it quickly dawned on me how long it would've taken me to save that amount of money had my dad not started for me that first year (and the years after that!). I realized that paying myself first was a very valuable life lesson—one that taught me the true value of being a relentless saver.

TO SAVE AND INVEST

One common characteristic of the multigenerationally

wealthy is their desire to save and invest. These concepts seem trivial, but they are truly important to wealth generation. As you saw in the previous chapter, saving means spending less than you earn. Investing means your hard-earned money is given to someone who will use it for an economically productive cause. It also involves taking risks in order to achieve a higher return for money you'll need at a later time.

There are a few useful concepts worth noting here:

- Start investing early and never stop—be relentless.
- There are countless investment philosophies, many of which may be successful.
- There are countless risks to investing, nearly all of which are difficult to predict. These risks should be minimized whenever possible, though they cannot be completely eliminated. Potentially catastrophic risks should be avoided.
- Although diversification does not guarantee a portfolio's protection, it may help lessen losses in volatile markets. The mathematics of retirement income planning favors the consistency of return rather than the magnitude of return.
- Your portfolio should be managed based on your goals and with your specific needs and risk profile in mind. The best portfolio for you is one you can stick with during good times and bad. Most investors have

a greater chance of sticking with a portfolio specifically designed to accomplish their goals.
- It's important to have an investment policy or strategy, preferably one with an academic basis. Investors
using a formal investment strategy tend to be more
confident in their convictions. This confidence helps
them maintain their portfolio during periods of negative returns.

Investment theories are like snowflakes; no two are alike.
But *how* you invest isn't nearly as important as starting
early and sticking with a game plan.

UNEMOTIONAL INVESTMENT

Every long-term investor will face both booms and busts.
Not surprisingly, the booms are accompanied by emotional highs and the busts are full of despair. Famed
investor Warren Buffett attributed some of his success
against emotional biases to his counterintuitive approach:
"We simply attempt to be fearful when others are greedy
and to be greedy only when others are fearful." Not only
are people less apt to invest when markets decline, they
are far more likely to want to sell their portfolios.

Managing your money isn't always about earning the
most; sometimes it's about managing risks to mitigate
losses. We all go through downturns, and two things can

be lost in investing: money and value. When you lose money, it's gone forever, and you have to make more. When you lose value, however, you have a chance to regrow. The goal is to lower the probability of complete monetary loss while accepting losses in value that you can eventually bounce back from.

In accomplishing multigenerational wealth, investors' goals shift away from doubling or tripling the portfolio value. Ultimately, as wealth increases, the goal becomes to prevent massive declines. Maintaining your direction comes with planning and focusing on your goals and reassessing them every couple of years. While your strategy will undoubtedly be tweaked periodically to keep up with the ever-changing global markets, you will constantly need to remain confident and focused on your goals.

Benjamin Graham stated, "Portfolio management is the management of risks, not the management of returns. All good portfolio management begins and ends with this process." When you tie an investment, savings, or wealth strategy to your goals, you are more apt to make better, more confident long-term decisions for yourself and your family.

Many years ago, I met with a prospective client who had nearly all her wealth in a single company's stock. This client, who we will call Ann, had divorced from a local business executive, and her share of the settlement was all she would have to live on. The stock had done well and was a primary contributor to their marital wealth. Her emotional attachment to the stock that had made so much money caused Ann to be hesitant to part with it.

I told her, "Your biggest risk is this company's stock, where you have nearly all your money invested. If its price declines to five dollars a share, you're going back to work."

"I don't want *that*," Ann said. "What do I do?"

We put together a plan to start liquidating her stock, and we entered orders to sell the stock at varying prices. The plan included taking the stock sale proceeds and reinvesting them into a more diversified portfolio that wasn't reliant on a single company. (Remember that diversification does not prevent portfolios from declining in value. Rather, it's designed to protect against major losses of capital from a single company or industry suffering major declines.)

At first, we sold the stock at twenty-two dollars a share. Then the stock climbed to twenty-four dollars, which upset Ann because she had sold some at the lower price. I encouraged her to stay the course and follow the plan we'd committed to, reminding her that she was reducing a major company-specific risk. We sold the next blocks of stock at twenty-six dollars and twenty-eight dollars a share. Each time the price rose, she was upset about the lower-priced sales and second-guessed her decision.

Then the 2008-2009 recession hit, and the stock Ann used to own plunged to nearly five dollars per share. Her discipline to stick with the plan of addressing a specific risk by selling off stock made the difference between remaining retired and having to go back to work. The stock had had a low likelihood of declining so much...yet it happened. If Ann had held the stock, she would have suffered life-changing consequences.

Situations like this happen far more often than you might think. A second set of eyes and ears may help you make less-emotional decisions.

INVESTOR BEHAVIOR

Understand ahead of time that enemy number one for any investor is human nature—and this is seen in a variety of investor behaviors. Economist Benjamin Graham said, "The investor's chief problem—even his worst enemy—is likely to be himself." Understanding your own behavior around financial planning may help you to avoid problems down the road.

Did you ever hear someone say, "I don't keep sweets in the house...I don't trust myself"? They understand their behaviors and do what they need to avoid the situation.

Too many business owners think, "I'll work and work and work, and then I'll sell my business and that'll be my retirement." That's the extent of their retirement planning. While this plan works for some, it can be disastrous for others. Most people find they need to do more than rely on the sale of their business. What if you were a GM dealer who said that during the Great Recession of 2008-2009?

One planning tool is what I call "monetizing your wealth." This simple advice means taking money out of your business and reinvesting it personally to plan for your future without the business. The goose will eventually die or transfer out of your care, and you want to prepare for when the golden eggs stop being laid.

One problem with monetizing your wealth is that it can be deceptively easy when times are good. The challenge comes when times are bad—you worry more and investment decisions become more nerve-racking, leading to rash decisions. As the *European Financial Review* observed, "More anxiety about an investment increases its perceived risk and lowers the level of risk tolerance among investors."[1] Think about walking across a six-inch-wide, ten-foot balance beam a foot off the ground... No problem, right? Suppose we move the balance beam thirty stories up and ask you to walk across...Not so easy, is it? Will you have the conviction and confidence to walk the plank with your chosen investment strategy? The emotional impact of potentially unpleasant outcomes makes decision making more difficult because they tend to alter investors' judgment.

This can be clearly seen in a financial advisor's office. When the markets are good, our phones don't ring. When markets and client portfolios decline, however, people suddenly call to make changes. They believe that something isn't working, and they want to stray from their strategy.

Having an academically based investment plan that you understand may help you combat these emotional urges. An investment philosophy that seems sensible and practical, and that you will follow, whether times are good or bad, is really important. Equally helpful is when you marry your investment plans to your long-term goals— and have the discipline to stick with it.

Discipline is the opposite of following fads or acting on

---

1   H. Kent Baker and Victor Ricciardi, " How Biases Affect Investor Behaviour," European Financial Review, February 28, 2014, http://www.europeanfinancialreview.com/?p=512.

emotions. It's about doing something because it's good for you, even if you wouldn't normally choose to do it. Discipline in investing is not much different from that of dieting, exercising, studying, or anything else. When you take money out of your business, have an automatic, unemotional plan for what you're going to do with it. If you have a system that adds money to your investment portfolio automatically, as you would a mortgage, the plan tends to work better. Human nature dictates that if you have to write the check, fill out the envelope, and lick the stamp, you're less likely to go through this process during hard times. Try to remove any and all emotional barriers and rely on professionals to help guide you through.

THERE IS NO "TOO SOON"

The bottom line is that you can't start saving and investing early enough. At the same time, you can't do anything about yesterday. You can, however, start fresh today, with your eyes on the goal line.

Saving involves relentless, unwavering passion and discipline; you need a goal. My goal is to retire with time and money for the activities I enjoy, like golf and family vacations. What does life after your business look like for you and your family?

You don't have to earn a lot of money to be a millionaire;

you just need to spend wisely and save religiously. The winningest golfers don't always have the most talent. They practice harder and smarter, surround themselves with the right caddy and coaches, and exhibit discipline in all facets of their lives. Their pursuit of golfing excellence is relentless—it's their sole focus.

You want coaches to help keep you focused and disciplined when the pressure is on. Multigenerational wealth planning is no different. Surround yourself with a caddy and cadre of coaches to make you the best you can be under pressure.

CHAPTER FIVE

PROTECTING IT

Guarding Your Hard-Earned Wealth

Finance is not merely about making money. It's about achieving our deep goals and protecting the fruits of our labor. It's about stewardship and, therefore, about achieving the good society.

—ROBERT J. SHILLER

On October 27, 2018, Vichai Srivaddhanaprabha, billionaire owner of the Leicester City Foxes Premier League soccer club, attended his team's soccer match. Afterward, as he did after most games, he boarded his private helicopter back to London. Unfortunately, the helicopter crashed soon after takeoff, killing everyone on board. One would think a man of his means would spare no expense for safety, yet something went terribly wrong.

On any given day, there is a newspaper story of someone who did not think yesterday would be their last day. Life is cruel in that way. It doesn't seem fair, but life rarely is. Both identifying the need and properly structuring your plans is a vitally important component of planning.

Some are prepared for the unforeseeables, while others are not. As a small business owner, you have three "parties" to worry about: (1) your company, including everyone who helps the goose thrive; (2) yourself, the business owner; and (3) your family. You need to be diligent in protecting yourself from as many potential problems as possible. Keep in mind that many of them may have a very low probability of occurring, yet they may have extremely high consequences. Many of these unforeseeable risks can be mitigated through insurance planning, yet many others need to be considered.

GUARD YOUR GOOSE

You will need to protect yourself against the actions of other people, accidents, acts of nature, and even changes to your health.

PROTECTION AGAINST THE ACTIONS OF OTHERS

The wealthier you are, the more you become a target for other people. Living in our litigious society, most business owners are familiar with minimizing exposure to lawsuits. While this is often done through insurance, it can also be done with proper legal advice and planning.

Today, business owners need to be concerned about more than just lawsuits. The mugger who used to hide in dark alleys now sits in front of a computer screen thousands of miles away. Cybercriminals may try to steal your personal identity and wealth without you even knowing it. They may try hacking your business as well. Your data is only as safe as your weakest link. Protecting your information and intellectual property from outsiders must become a personal and business priority.

Another area not often talked about is how to protect business assets from in-laws. Many business owners begin transferring their ownership interests to their children for estate-planning purposes. The last thing business owners want is having their business ownership interests caught in the middle of a divorce, potentially jeopardizing the business's future. Your legal counsel should be involved long before any potential problems might occur. Having a team member well-versed in both what can go wrong and how to protect you during this process may help mitigate problems in the event of a child's divorce.

PROTECTION AGAINST MISFORTUNE

Accidents can take place anywhere at any time. Fortunately, many risks can be passed on through proper insurance planning for *both* your business and your personal lives.

One aspect most are familiar with is property and casualty (P&C) insurance. Auto insurance and homeowner's coverage are the most common. Unfortunately, not all policies are created equal. There are a multitude of companies and ways to structure these policies, and many states mandate only a minimal amount of coverage. After your homeowner's and auto policies, there is additional coverage, excess liability, or umbrella policies that can provide additional protection. More recently, there are also policies to protect against identity theft. Find an experienced agent who can help structure a plan for you and review it every couple of years. P&C insurance is not a place to skimp.

The same goes for your business, yet it is more complicated. There are various types of business insurance (i.e., product liability, business interruption) that you may need. You cannot afford to jeopardize your entire business by having inadequate coverage due to a lack of planning. Again, this is expertise worth paying for.

Business owners tend to have "nicer" things, like pools,

airplanes, and boats. Each possesses varying degrees of risk and requires expertise to structure coverage. Insurance agents typically advise wealthy business owners to seek insurance coverage from companies specializing in these types of risks.

PROTECTION AGAINST MOTHER NATURE

All you have to do is turn on the news and you will see some sort of natural disaster taking place. These are generally low-probability, high-consequence events. Things like flood, fire, hail, sinkholes, and even earthquakes can be covered through insurance, both for your business and personal property. Proper planning means you should evaluate potential problems with your insurance professionals and periodically review coverage, as your insurance needs may change. Furthermore, you need a disaster plan to make sure your business can continue if you encounter such an event.

THE IMPORTANCE OF LEGAL COUNSEL

What most business owners may not consider in protecting their wealth is the importance of proper legal counsel. Your attorney's job is to protect your and your business's interests. The more they know about and understand your business, the better the advice you will most likely receive. While this involves properly structuring agreements and contracts, experienced legal counsel will help you identify some of the "unforeseeables." Lawyers' expertise can help you identify potential complications before they occur. They should be consulted through *all* stages of your planning. Yes, there is a cost for this type of relationship, but you need to consider it a small investment to protect you, the goose, and your family.

PROTECTION AGAINST HEALTH PROBLEMS

What happens if you become sick and can't take care of the goose? If your health fails, you have two potential issues: first, the day-to-day management of your business. Who will be minding the store? Do you have the appropriate legal documentation set up to allow someone to keep the business running? What if you can no longer come to work? Second, what happens to you and your family if you don't have any income? What if you encounter a longer-term illness? What if health issues force you to sell your business? Will your business valuation be significantly discounted if you "need" to sell? Having these foreseeable contingencies legally documented, planned, and properly insured is critical to your family's long-term planning.

Many potential health problems can be addressed through four primary types of insurance: health, life, disability, and long-term care (LTC). All four should be considered in your multigenerational wealth planning.

Health Insurance

This is probably the most familiar type of insurance, and it comes in many different styles and plans. There are also numerous ways to structure health insurance through your business. Having the proper guidance can make a difference in both the costs and benefits to you, your family, and your employees.

Life Insurance

Life insurance requires yet another type of expertise. Obviously, you should have adequate coverage that is coordinated between your business and personal lives. There are countless ways to structure your life insurance planning; but remember, engage experts early and continually reevaluate your plan. Remember, those who want life insurance the most are those who are not insurable. A little bit of planning can make a huge difference for your family.

Disability Insurance

Disability insurance protects your paycheck in the event you fall ill and are unable to work. As with other types of insurance, there are many ways for business owners to secure disability insurance through your business and personally.

The most important aspect of disability insurance is what

is called the "definition of disability," which defines the parameters upon which the insurance company deems you to be disabled. The best type of disability insurance is what is called "own occupation." This means the insurance company would provide a benefit (typically predetermined monthly payments until you turn age sixty-five) if you are unable to perform the specific duties of *your* occupation. Some disability policies have more restrictive definitions and may require you to work in another vocation.

For most business owners, their greatest asset is not their portfolio, but their ability to earn income. Protecting that income stream from disruption through disability insurance may be expensive, yet it is worth every penny if you someday need it. This is probably one of the most underutilized insurance planning areas.

Long-Term Care Insurance (LTCI)

Long-term care insurance is a fairly misunderstood planning tool. Many consumers overlook who it is designed to protect. LTCI is not about the person who may need care; instead, it's for the benefit of the caregiver, typically a spouse or family member. Yes, there is a significant financial benefit to LTCI, yet it is secondary.

For example, I have a number of clients who suffer from

dementia. Many of them receive professional care in memory units, happily spending time with people just like themselves. The true benefit of their LTCI is that it provides an infrastructure of care so that their spouses can maintain their lifestyles. Personally caring for someone in that condition is extremely stressful. There is an old saying that "people who care for chronically ill people become chronically ill themselves."

If you are considering LTC planning, think about the effects it would have on your spouse and your family and consider this an important aspect of your generational planning.

KNOW WHERE YOU'RE VULNERABLE

It's nearly impossible to objectively see everywhere you, your family, and your wealth may be at risk, so it's important to have expert insurance advisors who understand your situation and can help identify where you're vulnerable. A true wealth manager who understands you and your goals should coordinate these tasks between you and your expert team. You can purchase all the protection in the world, but if a thief or sue-happy person is able to find that one loophole, there may be little you can do to stop them. What protects your business also protects you. What protects you protects your family.

Only by making, saving, enhancing, and protecting your

wealth can you maximize the probability that you will have something to pass on to future generations. Chapter 6 contains the plays you may not have considered for Transferring It.

CHAPTER SIX

TRANSFERRING IT

Prepare Now to Maximize Wealth Transfer

The greatness of a man is not in how much wealth he acquires, but in his integrity and his ability to affect those around him positively.

—BOB MARLEY

Incidentally, the man whose name appears above, Bob Marley, is one of history's most famous celebrity estate-planning blunders. According to *Caribbean National Weekly*, Bob Marley "scoffed at the idea of a will, believing that such a document showed an inappropriate concern with earthly matters."[1]

---

1 "This Day in History: Bob Marley's Estate is Settled in Court," *Caribbean National Weekly*, December 9, 2015, https://www.caribbeannationalweekly.com/uncategorized/day-history-bob-marleys-estate-settled-court-left-family/.

Marley's estate was estimated to be about $30 million. On top of this, he apparently had some unsavory advisors found guilty of conspiracy in the management of his affairs.

You couldn't make this story up if you tried. This stresses the importance of properly planning your estate and surrounding yourself with trusted experts.

My clients tend to come to me saying that they've saved, they've spent wisely, they've made good financial decisions, and they're looking for someone to help perpetuate those decisions. Their ultimate goal is not just to spend money but to pass that wealth on to others—children, grandchildren, charities, nieces and nephews, and so on. In nearly every case, when I talk to couples, the financially minded spouse will say, "If something happens to me, I want my spouse taken care of." This typically means a well-thought-out plan is documented so if the unforeseen happens, the surviving spouse is not saddled with a huge burden or legal snafu.

Building wealth for your family is hard enough; passing it on to the next generation is even harder. The statistics on transferring wealth are not positive in terms of the amount that makes it to the second generation. According to a 2015 *Money* magazine article, "70 percent of wealthy families lose their wealth by the second generation, and a stunning 90 percent by the third."[2] It's a frightening reality for the generation that invested a lifetime and knows all the work that went into building wealth, only to see that money disappear with the next generation.

IT'S TIME TO TALK ABOUT WEALTH TRANSFER PLANNING

Nobody, whether a business owner or anybody else, likes talking about their demise. Combine that discomfort with your busy schedule, and it becomes all too easy to put off wealth transfer planning. Proper planning, however, increases the probability of perpetuated wealth, seeing it pass down to your children and eventually to your grandchildren.

Transferring a business or transferring wealth—or both— creates its own specific set of challenges. How do you treat each involved group equally? How do you decide what wealth to pass on and how much? The uniqueness of your individual business and the wealth it created means there are a lot of moving parts that need to be worked through. The anxiety of making mistakes, combined with the uncertainty most business owners feel, makes confident decision making a significant challenge. Having your plan stress-tested by someone who understands the

---

2   Chris Taylor, "70% of Rich Families Lose Their Wealth by the Second Generation," *Money*, June 17, 2015, http://time.com/money/3925308/rich-families-lose-wealth/.

uniqueness of your business and family dynamics could be extremely helpful. For example, if you have three children and one of them works in your business, how do you treat the other two? Most families believe that if they have three children, they have to treat them equally. If you give ten dollars to one child, you feel obligated to give ten dollars to each of the other two. But if you're in a situation where one child is in the business and the other two aren't, does the first child get treated differently? Many times, that child will buy the business at full fair market value, the same way anyone would.

In other cases, one of the three children spends eighty hours a week making the business better and increasing familial wealth. Meanwhile, the second and third children are on the company payroll as a way of redirecting money to create an element of equality. The question arises whether that child running the business should benefit financially more than the other two. As you might imagine, different business owners have different philosophies. You don't want to ruin your family dynamics over financial inequality among siblings, but you'd be surprised how often it happens.

One way to help yourself is with what we call the family meeting. This allows you to keep lines of communication open within your family. Get everyone together and talk through what values and goals are important to you and your spouse, and include your advisors. Don't let money ruin the family. While you can't predict what problems might arise, planning for these issues still provides a greater possibility of successfully handing off your business and your wealth while maintaining family harmony. More on family meetings appears later in the book.

Think back to Tiger Woods as he was preparing to make that fifteen-foot putt for the tie. Are you better off making the decision on your own or with a knowledgeable caddy behind you, helping gauge how much the putt's going to break?

An experienced wealth manager, an objective outsider, can play devil's advocate and challenge your planning ideas. They will make sure you are convinced your decision is right—think confidence. You need to challenge any decision you make and think about it from every possible angle. A lawyer does the same—always thinking about the other side.

Multigenerational wealth is a huge, complicated endeavor and it's different for every family. To keep it all in the family, business owners need two plans: an estate plan for their personal assets, and an estate plan for the business—what we call a succession plan. Let's take a look at what goes into the estate plan itself, once you have decided what will work best for your loved ones.

FOUR STEPS TO AN ESTATE PLAN

The first step of wealth transfer planning is called estate planning, and it's a critically important aspect of multigenerational wealth. An estate plan is not a one-and-done blueprint; instead, it is a living, breathing plan that must be updated and amended as your business and family situations change.

There are four steps involved in creating an estate plan: picturing your future, consulting with professionals, communicating clearly, and drafting your documents.

PICTURE YOUR FUTURE

You and your spouse must consider who you want to pass along your assets to and how much, if both of you are suddenly gone. At the outset, don't worry about taxes and transaction costs, because it may become too complicated. Next, consider the ramifications if only one of you were struck by lightning, while the other lives a full, long life. What will happen in the ideal scenario if *both* of you live a long time?

For business owners with children, this is where things can become complicated. Many small businesses are family-owned, to be passed on to the next generation. But how will the business be transferred? Will the process begin during your lifetime, or will it take place upon your passing? Many business owners have several children, often with one or more child not involved in the business. What if you are a doctor, lawyer, or architect whose business requires some professional certification? How will the wealth transfer to each child be handled?

In fairness to children not benefiting from the business, many business owners sell the business at fair market value to one or more of the children. Doing so allows the wealth to remain in the older generation, then to be passed down equally to their kids. Other business owners feel the children who work in the business should be allowed some "sweat equity." There is no right or wrong answer; the best plan is what works for your family and protects the relationships most effectively. Also, don't forget the benefits of properly communicating this among your family members.

For those without children, different types of decisions need to be made. What happens to the business if something happens to you? Will the proceeds go to charity or to an extended family member or partner? Who are the recipients of your bounty?

You're probably thinking that this is all rather complicated—and you're correct. Your job is simply to provide a clear breakdown of who should receive what. Perhaps you want to divide things into percentages, which makes logical sense to most people. Too many people procrastinate because they cannot decide to whom they will transfer their wealth. Don't let this be a stumbling block. Get some basic ideas on paper, then find an experienced estate-planning attorney to properly advise you of your options.

The most difficult part is getting your first plan in place. This makes the inevitable revisions far simpler. Understand that you will need to review and, perhaps, revise your plan every few years or as your personal/family dynamics change.

CONSULT WITH PROFESSIONALS

Once you have a basic idea of your dispositive scheme, then you need to create an estate plan. You need someone to identify the issues you face and to ask the right questions. Your attorney and CPA can provide legal and tax advice on options to help you accomplish your goals. Based on the complexity of your business structure, you may be able to both save on taxes and plan for catastrophic events—and you won't even need to recite the IRS tax code! The best estate-planning attorneys can boil the complex topics into simple terms you can understand. That's when you will be able to make sound long-term decisions for your wealth transfer goals.

Early in my brief legal career, a woman with three young children came to our firm. Her husband co-owned a business with two partners. The business had been growing nicely when the woman's husband died suddenly. There was a buy-sell agreement in place stating that the two remaining partners would purchase the business from the deceased partner's spouse. Despite all the proper planning, the two living business owners attempted to pay the widow less than she was entitled to, so she hired a lawyer, my boss.

One day, I was in his office when the lawyer for the surviving business partners called. What started as a peaceful conversation escalated into my boss raising his voice and ultimately screaming into the phone, complete with locker-room-caliber expletives. His final words to opposing counsel were "You had better get the right numbers together or we will be in court tomorrow."

He later told me that he didn't like to talk to people that way, but his duty was to protect his client—the widow with three young children. He was the only one who could stand up to the unscrupulous business partners who were trying to avoid paying what they truly owed her. My boss said, "One, that's just wrong; and two, she hired me to not let that happen." To this day, I am not sure she knew what happened in his office that day. This was one of the most valuable "aha" moments of my professional career.

This situation illustrates two points. First, even the best-laid plans go awry sometimes. Imagine if the couple had not planned. The situation would probably have been far worse. Ultimately, because of their planning, the problem was resolved and the widow received her fair share. Second, and equally important, is the value of having an advocate—someone who is *both* willing and capable of looking out for and protecting your interests. As a business owner, you will need many advocates to look after your affairs. These include financial, tax, and insurance advisors, and bankers. Choose them wisely; you never know when your family will need to count on them. Seek out a caddy and coaches who can help interpret the parameters of your planning during the drafting process and who will continue to make sure your plan remains up-to-date and matches your goals.

COMMUNICATE CLEARLY

One of the most underutilized and underappreciated tools for my clients' planning is plain old communication. Many times, we will facilitate this through a formal family meeting. We typically use this as an opportunity to share clients' plans with the next generation. Heirs get to meet me face-to-face, which is helpful as I explain what is being done and why. This is a great venue for parents to elaborate on how they've structured their plans, along with their expectations for their children. Including your advisors in this meeting is a sincere way to share your personal life story and the price you've paid for success. Then you can tie that into the wealth you've accumulated and how you'd like to perpetuate it for each generation. I've never heard a client wish their hard-earned wealth would be squandered within the next generation or two.

Up-front, open disclosure and conversation is a powerful tool to help alleviate future conflicts. Proper planning will forecast many potential problems and address them today. For extra measure, it is often beneficial to take notes during these planning meetings, so that everything is documented in writing.

A few years ago, an attorney told me a story about a family that disagreed about who should receive the family heirloom grandfather clock. The fair market value of the clock was only a few thousand dollars. Several of the children thought they should have it, so they decided to fight it out in the courts. After several years of litigation, the kids exhausted their parents' $7 million estate...on legal fees. The ultimate beneficiaries became the attorneys they employed. This is a problem that may have been prevented with some simple communication. Could this have been mitigated with proper communication and a family not ruined?

Of course, family meetings can be difficult when family

members hear things they don't want to hear. Unfortunately, many things in life worth doing are also the most difficult; however, they are often also the most rewarding. Do yourself a favor and meet with your family to discuss how your assets will be divided.

These conversations can be easier with a moderator, often your wealth manager. It's also important to introduce your kids to your professional advisors, who will help ensure that your children have the necessary support and your long-term financial interests in mind.

DRAFT YOUR DOCUMENTS

The final task is to draft and execute the necessary legal documentation. Unfortunately, it's difficult to avoid the need for some "legalese" during this process, but it's important that you understand how and why your assets are to be divided.

Estate planning generally includes three documents: a will, financial power of attorney, and healthcare power of attorney.

Most people are familiar with a will, which details your dispositive scheme and directs who will inherit what. It also names your executor, who will be in charge of managing your estate. Equally important are your beneficiary designations on assets such as retirement plans, IRAs, annuities, and life insurance.

> A critically important fact to understand is that beneficiary designations supersede your will. For example, if your will says everything goes to your spouse, yet you name your children as beneficiaries of your life insurance, the kids will get the life insurance proceeds. Your spouse will not. This is a very common misunderstanding and a mistake many people make.

Financial powers of attorney name a person who can handle your affairs. While they can be very limited in their scope, for estate-planning purposes, they are typically written to provide very broad powers to an agent in whom you must have complete trust. Typically, spouses are listed as agents, and sometimes children are named as backups in the event of death or disability.

Healthcare powers of attorney are very similar but authorize someone to make your healthcare decisions in the event you are unable to do so. They also usually include living will provisions for your end-of-life decisions. Healthcare and financial powers of attorney can be combined as a single document.

Too often, business owners spend the time, energy, and money to get everything drafted, but then they fail to sign the documents. Or they put the documents in a safe place and never look at them again. These documents should be reviewed along with your goals every two or three years. Part of the caddy's job is to make sure you consistently review these documents.

Remember, once a plan is in place, it, typically at least, can be easily modified. Think of it like your home: it takes a really long time to design and build, but once it is standing, you may just need to maintain it and redecorate it once in a while.

THE BEST-LAID PLANS

Even the most astute businesspeople make estate-planning blunders. One famous example involved the 85 percent owner of the NFL's Miami Dolphins back in the mid-1990s. The team's owner, Joe Robbie, wanted to pass the team on to his family. Unfortunately, he failed to account for the fact that federal estate tax would have to be paid on the value of the team.

Because the estate lacked the necessary cash to pay the tax, the family had to sell their 85 percent share to Wayne Huizenga for $109 million. The family then had to write a $43 million check for the tax bill. In 2009, Huizenga sold 95 percent of the team for a substantial profit, one that Mr. Robbie's family was not able to enjoy.

That was not the only price the family paid. *Sports Illustrated* reported, "But the Robbies paid a price too. As Diane, the oldest child, put it: 'This whole thing has destroyed [our] family.'"[3]

What are the real risks to *your* family for failing to plan?

The importance of having an estate plan, both for your personal assets and for your business, is inestimable. It can be the difference between your family thriving and struggling to survive. Planning might be different if end-of-life only happened to certain people, but we will all need it someday. No one, including myself, is getting out of this world alive.

Now that you understand your personal estate plan, let's take a look at what happens when the goose outlives you. You're going to need a succession plan.

WHAT IF THE GOOSE OUTLIVES YOU?

Although it is a bleak thought, you have to consider very real questions: *What if today is my last day? What do I want and need to happen?* You need estate planning for your business as well. You will have to identify and document

3   Michael Rosenberg, "The Super Bowl That Tore a Family Apart, Forever Changed Stadium Deals," *Sports Illustrated*, November 23, 2015, https://www.si.com/nfl/2015/11/24/miami-dolphins-super-bowl-joe-robbie-stadium.

who will own the business and try to maximize its value so your family can benefit after you are gone. Remember the woman with the three young children? How is the price to be determined? How is that person going to buy the business, and how much are they going to pay? Will they have to pay right away, or can they pay over time? All of these things need to be considered. There are basic business strategies for accomplishing this, but you need answers to these questions before you can document them with your attorney.

In addition, someone must be authorized to run day-to-day operations and pay the bills, and they must have your employees' and family's best interests at heart. Too often, small businesses rely totally on their owners as the sole decision-makers who hold all the details of daily operation in their head. If this is the case with your business, the goose may die with you.

To avoid this, you will want to have a succession plan in place. This might include selling your business or transferring it to your spouse or children. Perhaps your spouse will own the business and the kids will manage it and ultimately buy it.

If you haven't made arrangements, however, and your company is left to fend for itself, your competitors will waste no time contacting your clients or customers.

Several years ago, I was at our corporate headquarters when I ran into someone from our succession planning department. He said, "Did you know Joe died this week?" Joe owned a nearby financial advisory practice, like mine, and had died unexpectedly. I was asked if we wanted to purchase his practice, seeing as he didn't have a succession agreement. Due to securities laws, his spouse, who was not a registered securities person, could neither take over as owner, nor receive any ongoing payments from it. His widow collected nothing from his years of hard work. What is even more disturbing is that we have a department specializing in succession planning, which notifies branches to create and update succession plans. Joe definitely had all the resources and professional assistance, easily accessible, to protect his wife and family!

If you don't have a succession plan, you risk the demise of your company. When your succession plan is in place, be proactive about sharing your succession plan with your customers. Introduce them to the next leaders in line and assure them your business will run smoothly without you. This may seem basic, but you might be surprised how few business owners do this.

When it comes to creating your succession plan, start with the end in mind. How do you maximize the goose's value to your successor and maintain it as a profitable entity for the future? Then consider how your family can benefit from the value you've created, as tax-efficiently as possible. The more your successor is able to profit, the more your family should profit as well.

FEATURE YOUR FAMILY

How do you want your money and your business to benefit your spouse and children? If your spouse is financially minded or is involved in the business, it's likely that these discussions have already started. Your spouse may be equipped to handle much of the aftermath but will still benefit from the support of your advisors. Again, far too often, nonfinancial spouses exclude themselves from the planning due to a lack of interest. As much as they may not like it, they should be involved in both the big picture decision-making process and the basics of what planning is in place.

If your spouse is not involved, you need to know whether they'll be able to run the business if anything happens to you. Will they have to sell the business? What assets from the business can they count on receiving?

Another consideration is whether your spouse can handle all the money. Can they find a coach to help, or is there already one in place? In situations where the husband is the business owner, wives sometimes call advisors to secure help managing their wealth if their husband should die. Husbands sometimes call to make sure their wife will have help when the time comes. Even if there's written documentation in place, have you confirmed that it includes an actionable plan for your spouse or family members?

An up-and-coming trend that warrants consideration is that of women-owned businesses. According to a 2017 American Express report, "There are an estimated 11.6 million women-owned businesses in the United States that employ nearly 9 million people and generate more than $1.7 trillion in revenues."[4]

Stay-at-home dads or "house husbands" are more and more prevalent. This might be good news for legal, tax, and financial advisors. Based on observations from my first book, *What Now: A Widow's Guide to Financial Independence*, there were notable differences in how women plan versus how men plan. Women tend to be better at planning than men because they are better at considering advice and working out a viable solution with the guidance of those who advise them. They are more apt to listen to their caddy and coaches and follow through on tasks; then they can focus their time and energy on taking care of the goose.

---

4   *The 2017 State of Women-Owned Businesses Report*, American Express, http://about.
    americanexpress.com/news/docs/2017-State-of-Women-Owned-Businesses-Report.pdf

Finally, you have to consider your expectations for how your children will manage your business and wealth when it is their turn to do so.

Years ago, I had a client with pancreatic cancer. One day, she called to say the doctor had given her ninety days to live. With such a short amount of time left, I suggested we tackle the estate planning she had ignored the previous five years. My client's daughter was the sole beneficiary. The adult daughter spent hours watching television and compulsively buying goods from home shopping shows. She had a room full of unopened boxes; she couldn't even remember what she'd bought.

My client expressed concern about leaving money to her daughter to spend frivolously. She considered creating a trust to control the disposition of her assets over time to her daughter. Her concern was that even if she put the money in a trust, the daughter could hire an attorney who could find a way to get the money and spend it. Today, I truly believe my client delayed her estate planning because she did not know what to do, so she did what is so common—she did nothing.

In the end, she decided that her daughter's actions were her own responsibility, and to leave the money to her free of trust. The daughter found lots of creative ways to spend the money, and it was gone in only a few years.

You only have so much control over how the money you leave is spent. Greater wealth does afford you more planning opportunities, such as generational trust planning, yet spendthrift children pose unique and difficult challenges. You can customize your plan according to your values and goals, but once you're gone, those left behind are in control of their actions and decisions. For many who choose to use trusts in their planning, the benefits to their family can be invaluable.

CONSIDER CHARITABLE GIVING

A common theme among successful business owners is their human desire to give back to the world at large. Incidentally, the Internal Revenue Code provides incentives for those charitably inclined. Understand that no one donates money to enjoy tax benefits; nonetheless, proper planning may result in lower taxes for you and your family.

Several years ago, a client wanted to do just that. He was a very wise saver and investor who inherited money from his parents who were the same way. One of his primary goals was to give back.

As we discussed what he wanted to accomplish, we viewed various options to direct monies to various charities. He had a significant amount of highly appreciated stock, meaning that if he sold it, he would have had to pay capital gains tax on the profits.

Instead of writing a check, he was able to give the actual shares of stock to the charities, meaning he would not have to pay capital gains tax. He then received a substantial tax deduction. As an offset to this income tax deduction, he was able to then convert a portion of his IRA to a Roth IRA, meaning the money would potentially grow tax-free for his lifetime and perhaps beyond (provided he met various IRS requirements).

A number of charitable giving techniques are available and all depend on your particular situation. That's why planning is so important. What's good for you may not help your neighbor.

Early in my career, a wealthy woman in her seventies was trying to determine how her estate would be distributed. She had no children and planned to pass her wealth on to several cousins. Since she and my father had a strong long-term relationship, he understood her goals and what she wanted to accomplish. When my father and her attorney asked who was most important to her, these family members never came up.

Then it occurred to her to give her money to a charity she believed in. "Is that allowed?" she asked.

"Of course," my father replied, much to her relief.

She'd just assumed she should give money to her relatives, but was thrilled to choose a group of people who were more closely in line with her personal values.

The law allows you to pass on your wealth to anyone you choose. Whoever that may be, you must make difficult decisions to identify them and determine how to structure those bequests to make sure their value will be maximized. The more people you include, the greater the chance of problems arising later.

Charitable planning is important to many successful entrepreneurs. A detailed description of charitable gifting is beyond the scope of this book, but it is important to note that if you plan to give wealth to charities, get advice now to maximize those tax benefits.

Additionally, consider gifting to charities while you are alive. Again, you may experience immediate income tax benefits while also seeing the reward of your gift. If you want to give your church a new stained-glass window, wouldn't you rather do so while you are alive to enjoy it?

Once again, making sure someone is asking you the right questions is important as you make decisions about where your wealth will go.

KNOW WHEN TO SELL

There are times when selling a business is the best option for an owner and their family. For most professional businesses requiring specific expertise, such as the practices of doctors, lawyers, dentists, and engineers, your family may not have the skillset or designations to succeed you. In other situations, the spouse or children may simply not want to run the business. As discussed above, a large part of planning is communicating with your family to determine whether they are interested in continuing to run your company after you.

If there is no family to take on the role of owner, start thinking today about a suitable successor. This may be an employee or even a competitor, but should be someone who can profitably take over your business. Greed can kill such a deal, so be flexible and generous. Perhaps assume some risk through an earn-out where both you and the buyer can mutually succeed. Most business owners want their business to continue prospering in the future. Wouldn't you?

Regardless, start thinking about the future of your business today. Life will change, but any plan is better than no plan at all. If you have a buyer for your business or a buy-sell agreement, you help maximize the value for your heirs. You also provide security for your employees and their families. They tend to be more comfortable and, as a result, more productive when they know their paychecks will continue uninterrupted.

The value of John Doe, Inc. now is almost always greater than trying to sell John Doe, Inc. the day after his funeral. Who is going to pay full price for something someone has to sell in a hurry or under duress?

TAX EFFICIENCY IS A MOVING TARGET

Once you have landed upon someone to benefit from your succession plan, you will need to explore the various ways to transfer assets, some of which are more tax efficient than others. A business might be transferred intergenerationally, from parents to children. Sometimes assets pass better through the business; other times they pass better through outside methods, such as life insurance, ESOPs, or gifting. These options vary drastically by company and require special expertise in tax and corporate law. Surrounding yourself with the proper professionals is critical.

Someone once told me, "The older you get, the faster time goes by." Unfortunately, he seems right. When it's time to trade in a new car, doesn't it feel like you just bought it? When you look at a picture of your children, doesn't it seem like yesterday they were that young? Time flies when you're having fun. From a planning standpoint, as time evolves, several things happen. One certainty is that tax laws will change, and the way they change is difficult to predict. Typically, it's best to draft documents based on current tax laws. Then, have your tax and legal counsel review these documents periodically to avoid a huge mistake if the laws change, which they inevitably will.

Most business owners are not aware of how tax laws will affect them directly, so you should get assistance. Every time you update these documents, place a meeting date in your calendar a couple of years in the future as a reminder to revisit them. You should also review your corporate bylaws and succession plans each year, and assign someone to be accountable for making sure this happens.

WHAT POSITIVE WEALTH TRANSFER LOOKS LIKE

Positive experiences of wealth transfers are absolutely possible. With the right guidance and a solid plan, it can be a fairly smooth process. Let me share some examples so you can see for yourself what that looks like.

A PARTNERSHIP

A very successful business owner was used to doing the heavy lifting to grow his business himself. Several decades ago, he began to realize that he needed help managing the dramatic growth his company was experiencing. His solution was to hire a few local businessmen to help him run the business. These were men who shared his values and vision, and he knew he could trust them to make important decisions for the company and for his family. Though he maintained the final say on important decisions, they met almost daily to brainstorm and talk through any pressing issues the business was facing.

As time evolved, the owner relied more and more on this team for everything, and the business did nothing but grow. As the owner aged, he became less and less involved in the business's day-to-day operations. Fortunately, decades before, he had empowered his close-knit and loyal team to carry on the business as he would have wanted. That was his succession plan; he didn't know when it would be needed, but the impact to his family could have been catastrophic. Even after the owner passed on, the business continued to flourish under his remaining business partners.

These men were the business owner's succession plan, undertaken decades before it was needed. He surrounded himself with intelligent people who upheld and continued to run the business by specific standards set by the owner and his family.

He hired wise people to work with him. You may not have a business large enough to do that, but you can still apply the mindset of growing your business well after you are no longer able to. If someone else can't take care of the goose, then the goose may die with you. But you want the goose to live well beyond your years, laying as many eggs as possible to benefit you and your family. Great businesses survive their owners.

A MOTHER'S NEEDS

Years ago, a prospective client's daughter contacted me in the hope of solving some of her investment and estate problems. The mother was in her nineties and had accumulated substantial assets in just a few healthcare companies' stocks. The mother's health was simply not as good as it used to be, and dementia was setting in. The daughter thought she needed professional advice.

Due to her increasing cognitive issues, the mother faced potentially significant long-term-care bills. Her daughter was also concerned about her lack of diversification. My recommendation was to build a plan with her eldercare attorney and to work in conjunction with her CPA. The daughter was all in and just wanted to delegate investment, legal, and tax advice to a team of professionals.

The eldercare attorney was able to provide options to solve most of the family's problems. He recommended updating the mother's estate-planning documents and creating two separate trusts. This planning helped minimize income and inheritance taxes, while also providing a solution to sell some of her stock holdings. The CPA agreed with the strategy and the plan was put in motion.

Within several months the plan was in place, yet it would require periodic monitoring. Until the mother's passing, the daughter met with the CPA twice each year: once for planning and the other for tax return preparation. She also consulted annually with the attorney to make sure the plan still functioned from a legal standpoint and to see if any changes were necessary. The daughter could focus her efforts on caring for her mother, knowing she had professionals to rely on.

Wait, you might be saying. *Doesn't this cost more?* Certainly it does. What's the value to the daughter to have a team of professionals working together for the family's benefit? Only she can answer that question.

Very few people would go to the lengths the daughter did to protect both her mother and her mother's assets in the hope of maximizing the benefit to the entire family. This is the type of diligence required for proper multigenerational wealth planning.

SOUND LIKE A PLAN?

You've got your game plan for making and keeping your money, enhancing it, protecting it, and transferring it. When it comes time to pass your business on, you have the right people in place to make your estate and succession plans a success. So, where should you focus your energies? Doing what only *you* can do: running your personal, unique, specific business as the quarterback of your business. Then enlist your team of advisors who can not only serve as coaches to help navigate any issues that arise, but also provide thoughtful, professional advice. Easier said than done? Perhaps, but part 3 will show you how to find a caddy that can lead to success on and off the field.

PART THREE

FINDING FINANCIAL CADDIES WHO FIT THE BILL

Everyone needs a coach. It doesn't matter whether you're a basketball player, a tennis player, a gymnast, or a bridge player.

—BILL GATES

For nearly every business owner, myself included, the next-highest-paying career is considerably less than your current one. Think about a Major League Baseball player who earns $20 million per year. If he can no longer play baseball due to injury or retirement, it's unlikely he'll find another job with similar pay. While he is playing, his sole focus should be playing at the sport's highest level. He most likely outsources all his other duties, hiring nutritionists, trainers, agents, financial advisors, insurance agents, and attorneys. Why would he try to take on these duties when he's not an expert at them and they take time away from practicing his craft? In the same thinking, why would you spend your time on anything but your business?

The specialization of today's businesses requires constant focus, reinvention, and continuing evolution in one form or another. That is a full-time job and then some. An old business coach once told me to pick three things I do best and hire someone else to do everything else—and I listened to him. Everything in my life improved, from my business to my family to my health (my wife even started liking me again!). I don't prepare my own taxes, write my own estate plan (even though I'm able to), or procure my P&C insurance. For each of those time-consuming tasks, I've engaged trusted professionals who specialize in doing those very things. At times, I've had to make the difficult decision to replace some of these professionals in favor of more expertise. Sure, they cost money, but like many of you, my business is my most important asset. Why would I want to divert energies to anything else?

Multigenerational wealth requires the attention and expertise of people focused on your and your family's goals. Business owners like you need to surround yourself with a team of professionals whose expertise can be leveraged to accomplish your goals. That leaves you more time and energy to care for the goose.

You may think that you can read up; take courses in investment, tax, and estate planning; and figure it out on your own. And you're probably correct. The internet has tools enabling you to do legal documents, taxes, and investments, all saving you money. However, the internet is not likely to show you the right questions to ask. Doesn't it make more sense to have coaches who will boil down legalese, investment guidance, tax regulations, and other issues in terms you can understand? Then you can make even more sound, practical, long-term decisions to help you achieve multigenerational wealth.

Think back to the professional golfer analogy at the US Open. If that were you, would you hire a caddy to carry your bag and interpret all the advice of your other professionals (your swing coach, psychologist, and fitness coaches) on the field of play? Every swing is an irrevocable decision, just like in your business, so you need to make sure you have proper advice for each one. That's where wealth advisors like me come in—we're your financial caddy. The right advisor will take the time to understand you, your family, and your goals. You and your spouse will be asked the right questions so you can explore and define your goals. You will define what you want to do and, more importantly, what you need to address to achieve those goals. You should better understand not only where you are today and where you want to go, but also how to get there.

Why is this so valuable? If you can outsource your wealth management planning, you accomplish a couple of things. You associate yourself with a professional whose sole interest is in you attaining your, and your family's, goals. This is a team member, much like your most valued employees who keep your business running smoothly. Besides help with your investment planning, you have a relationship manager to coordinate your legal, tax, and insurance planning.

When you have a major strategy meeting at your company,

don't you include the IT person along with operations and sales? You want all major decisions coordinated. Wealth management is no different. Communication between your various professionals often lessens the likelihood of mistakes. Wealth managers coordinate this for you, much like a caddy does on the course for the golfer.

In the chapters that follow, you will learn not only how your caddy can help you, but how you can ask the right questions of both yourself and potential advisors. Sometimes, when you know what you are looking for, it becomes easier to find it.

CHAPTER SEVEN

A SPECIALIZED
AND HOLISTIC
APPROACH

"Would you tell me, please, which way I ought to go from here?"

"That depends a good deal on where you want to get to," said the Cat.

"I don't much care where—" said Alice.

"Then it doesn't matter which way you go," said the Cat.

"—so long as I get SOMEWHERE," Alice added as an explanation.

"Oh, you're sure to do that," said the Cat, "if you only walk long enough."

—LEWIS CARROLL, *ALICE IN WONDERLAND*

The world is becoming more specialized, and it's getting to be more difficult to be an expert in any one thing, let alone two or three different areas.

A few years ago, a friend—an orthopedic surgeon—had to take his daughters to urgent care because they were sick. I asked him why he would need to go to urgent care when he's a doctor. He said, "I'm an orthopedic surgeon. I don't know anything about caring for kids' illnesses. I've forgotten all that basic stuff from medical school." He's a spine surgeon, so his knowledge is highly specialized to that area of medicine. He wouldn't operate on someone with an ankle injury or shoulder problem; he would send them to an ankle or shoulder specialist.

Your business also requires specialized knowledge. The more successful your business becomes, the more important it is for you to stay focused. When hiring a new employee, isn't the goal to find someone who can leverage your time to build your business? Shouldn't you find advisors who do the same thing for your multigenerational wealth? Of course.

People drastically underestimate how difficult managing

long-term wealth can be. The world is full of self-help books and financial TV shows trying to convince you otherwise. This chapter will expand upon just how much goes into managing wealth, from understanding the roles of your different advisors, to finding the right fit, and recognizing the questions you will be asked as your caddy tries to set a game plan to help you navigate the course... of life.

THE ROLE OF A TRUE WEALTH MANAGEMENT ADVISOR

When working with your advisors to make legal, tax, and financial decisions, you will discuss highly intimate life details: your hopes, goals, and dreams; the wins and losses of your past decisions; and the ways in which you want to care for your family after you're gone. This level of intimacy is necessary in order for your advisors to fully understand your goals and your intended purpose for your wealth. This means you will have to divulge the good, bad, and ugly aspects of your family. Nobody's perfect, and neither is anyone's family. You'll discuss with advisors what you wouldn't tell anyone else. It is highly personal, and that's what makes it so valuable.

Your advisors should have a deep understanding of tax, legal, and financial principles. They should know the rules of the game and how you can apply those rules to benefit yourself and your family. Think about this: would you rather have advisors with all the answers or advisors who have all the right questions to ask you? They should also work together, understanding how all their different personalities will contribute to the dynamics of managing your unique situation.

The right advisors for you will assess the facts, apply your goals, and ultimately formulate strategies with your entire family's best interests in mind. Because many of these issues are so complex, your advisors will need to break down the issues into bite-sized chunks so you can understand their application. You cannot make sound decisions on matters you don't completely understand. You need the confidence that you are making the best long-term decisions. Then, you can begin to solve your planning problems one at a time. When an advisor can present your options in clear conversation, point for point, you're better able to make educated decisions for the best ways to proceed. That's the art of multigenerational wealth planning. While there's a lot of financial "science" involved, there's an art to it too.

There's a necessary balance between working with a knowledgeable advisor and utilizing your advisor's knowledge to become an educated and active part of the decision-making process. It's an integral piece of making choices about wealth transfer.

To continue to impress the importance of this point—confident decisions are based on wise counsel. But how do you know if the counsel you seek is the wisest, or best, person for the job?

THE SIX CS

The best advisors help in three ways:

- They encourage you to look at a problem or opportunity from multiple angles.
- They help you balance the tug of the short term with important long-term priorities.
- They ask the tough questions you need to consider—but may not know to ask—in order to reach the best solution.

Super-wealthy families create what are called "family offices." According to *Forbes*, "a family office should be able to provide for tax compliance work, access to private banking and private trust services, document management and recordkeeping services, expense management, bill paying, bookkeeping services, family member financial education, family support services, and family governance."[1] These wealthy families see the value in hiring their own team of advisors to help with their mul-

---

1   Todd Ganos, "What Is a Family Office?" *Forbes*, August 13, 2003, https://www.forbes.com/sites/toddganos/2013/08/13/what-is-a-family-office/#3e3dff1fa13f.

tigenerational wealth planning. Because few people have *that* level of resources, the trend today is for successful business owners to hire a wealth manager who coordinates their affairs within their own mini-family office.

Once you recognize the value of doing so, and realize that you need help in these areas, how do you find the right advisor? The best way is to know what you are looking for.

From talking with many affluent business owners, I've gleaned a set of guiding principles, the "Six Cs," for finding the right financial caddy:

CHARACTER

Character involves doing what you say you're going to do. Does the person you're considering as a caddy know how to follow through? Will this advisor provide the ongoing advice and services you need? Will they ask you the right questions?

CHEMISTRY

You need to get along with the person who is going to deep-dive into your goals and finances. Ask yourself, "Do I like this person? Is this advisor someone I would like to spend time with and share some of my innermost emotional and financial problems?" It can be difficult to find someone with whom you have chemistry, so take the time you need to find the right fit.

CARING

Three-quarters of life is caring. If someone works hard and cares about you, your family, and your financial future, they're automatically among your best options. You know when someone cares, and that concern goes a long way—especially when you face a major problem and you really need help.

COMPETENCE

Obviously, competence involves having the necessary credentials and experience. In addition, this advisor must be committed to staying informed of the latest developments and changes in laws, regulations, and opportunities. Experience brings the gift of wisdom, but an astute advisor stays ahead of the game and pays attention to the evolving landscape of financial planning.

COST EFFECTIVENESS

Financial planning isn't something you want to skimp on, because you often get what you pay for. At the same time, however, you don't want to be gouged. Understand the costs ahead of committing to a specific advisor. Costs are only high in the absence of value, and only you can value whether the expense is worthwhile for you and your family. There's a saying, "You can't put a price on good advice," which is even more important during tough times.

CONSULTATIVE

You want someone on your side of the table. Business owners want advice about both their options and solutions to their problems. Business owners don't seem to want someone who simply sells products; they want someone to spot issues that may adversely affect them. These typically arise from open and honest communication about yourself, your family, and your business.

FIND THE BALANCE

Looking at the Six Cs, your dream caddy may seem nearly impossible to find. You should determine which of the Cs are most important to you; each will have to be balanced against the other.

Keep in mind that many successful advisors will be gauging you with the same metrics. Not every potential client is a good fit for them, Many advisors view "ideal" clients as those who share a host of common traits. Those who are willing to accept advice (being coachable) and those willing to do what it takes to be successful are highly regarded. If you were a caddy, what type of golfer would you want to work with?

Most business owners look at chemistry as most important. Communication is naturally intertwined, but most will say that speaking in simple terms is high on the list. Competence is table stakes for any advisor dealing with the affluent, especially business owners. What might be surprising to you is that cost is less often an issue when business owners feel they've made the right choice. Balance what is important to you to help guide your decision.

QUESTIONS BEFORE ANSWERS

When I was a young attorney, an older attorney once told me, "Son, you probably think you'll be a great attorney when you have all the answers, but that just isn't true. You'll be a great attorney when you know all the right questions to ask."

If you decide to consult with a wealth manager, don't expect to simply show up with a folder of financial statements and get immediate investment advice. Instead, expect to gather a substantial amount of financial information, including tax returns, estate-planning documents, and life insurance, along with all of your financial statements. These are necessary for the advisor to fully understand where your plan is today. Then, expect to be asked a series of questions, most of which are extremely personal.

You will entertain questions about things you've never considered. You might be surprised how often a husband and wife of several decades say to each other, "I never knew that about you." Expect to field questions such as "What are your goals for your business? What's important to you and your family? What do you and your family want to accomplish with your money?" This initial meeting should be designed for you and your advisor to get to know each other and to identify your big-picture goals, along with some of the hurdles you face. It's harder to accomplish your goals if they haven't been documented.

A prospective client and his wife were once introduced to me by one of my clients. He was in his midsixties and wanted to retire at age seventy. As he answered the long line of questioning, it quickly became apparent that he would need about 2.5 times his current investment base to accomplish his goals. He spent more than he earned, including using his retirement plan to pay for his kids' education. In my opinion, he needed to truly understand that his lifestyle was unsustainable.

His final question to me was "How much time is this going to take?" My immediate response was that it was going to require a substantial commitment to properly plan because he and his wife would need to carefully consider a host of really difficult long-term decisions. He didn't want to make that commitment, and quite frankly, I could not help him—the math just didn't work. If multigenerational wealth is your goal, you'll need to make a meaningful time investment.

Someone asking the right questions draws out your pain points, strengths, and weaknesses to understand your situation and be able to provide objective advice. That's what allows you to attain those dreams—and that can be very powerful. There's an art to asking questions, and a question-asking structure allows a professional to learn a lot about you and your family in a short period of time. Most times, a particular answer raises several more questions to fully define your needs. The better they know you and your situation, the more apt you are to get sound advice.

SEVEN CATEGORIES OF QUESTIONS

To help illustrate the importance of probing questions, let me introduce what my firm and I call our Wealth Management Consultative Process, which we use at our unique Discovery Meeting. During this time, we ask a series of thoughtful questions designed to help us get to know you, your goals, what and who is important to you, and how you value money. Another goal of this meeting is to determine whether we are a good fit for you, and whether you are a fit for us.

These questions fall into seven categories of focus:

1. *Financial Values:* What's important to you about money? This is the first question we ask every new prospective client, and it's open-ended by design. Money means different things to different people. The way you answer this question begins to form the basis for documenting your longest-term goals. Until you elaborate on and understand what is important to you about money, formulating your financial goals is impossible.

2. *Personal, Professional, and Family Goals:* Many of our clients are what we call "family stewards," the matriarchs or patriarchs of the family. Their goals tend to focus on their families, even more than on themselves. We probe deeply to help identify what you want to accomplish with your wealth and how that will impact all facets of your life.

3. *Relationships:* In many cases, these significant people are family, but sometimes others are included. Some clients have connections with their church or alma mater. Documenting your closest personal and family relationships is important for your long-term planning and wealth transfer.

4. *Assets:* These questions establish where your wealth is located and how to value it. The focus of most successful business owners is to retire comfortably and maintain their lifestyle. After that, they want to manage their wealth to efficiently pass it on to succeeding generations. A significant emphasis must be placed on which assets to use for retirement and which are more appropriate for wealth transfer. Developing a comprehensive plan begins with a comprehensive assessment. Many new clients come to me looking for a "stress test" of their portfolios and their plans to make sure they are covering all the bases with their planning.

5. *Advisors:* Enlisting the right team around you, and making sure everyone works together, is vital. I typically act as a liaison between you and your other professional advisors. They almost always include lawyers and accountants, but also may include bankers, insurance agents, and business consultants. These questions are designed to make sure you fully leverage those relationships to get valuable advice as you move toward multigenerational wealth. Doing so also allows you to focus energy on your family and the goose.

6. *Process:* These questions are designed to establish your expectations of how you want to work together. Some business owners want to be involved in every step along the way, while others prefer to delegate. An

up-front discussion of what to expect and an under-standing of how the relationship will evolve is helpful to most clients. This line of questioning identifies business owners who are truly interested in achieving their goals. It also delineates family members they want involved in their planning, either now or some-time down the road.

7. *Personal Interests:* This is the fun part. We get to talk about all your personal interests and what you do in your free time. People's favorite hobbies and even sports teams become really important in their lives. Believe it or not, this is an important part of the long-term relationship.

The details discovered through these questions—what drives people, what makes them tick, what's important to them, how they spend their time—are the foundation of your planning. When a goals-based multidisciplinary plan is created, you are more likely to accomplish what you set out to do. It also increases the chances that your plan weathers the inevitable bumps in the road we all face in life. Perhaps that sounds simple—and it should, because it is...with the right guidance.

ALIGNING YOUR *WHY*

Certain financial topics are fun to discuss; others aren't. Enjoyable or not, they are all integral to crafting your future wealth plans. A Discovery Meeting allows people to answer questions openly and honestly in a purely conversational setting, without feeling threatened. Most everyone finds the exercise both interesting and rewarding. You would be surprised how much we learn when completing this exercise.

Discovery also allows you to better understand yourself, your spouse, and ultimately your goals. When decisions are based on your most important goals, you have a better understanding of the actions that must be completed. Too often, people nod their heads but fail to understand the pros and cons of their decisions. The more clients understand their problems, the more defined their goals become and the more dramatically their confidence increases. Goals-based decision making is quite valuable. When you know the *why* behind your aspirations and actions, you can see the logic and rationality that will help you make better decisions.

In my early days of coaching basketball, I tried to teach kids to dribble with their nondominant hand. They wouldn't do it properly. I decided to ask if they knew why this was so important. No one had an answer. I then showed them live examples of what happens when they dribble the wrong way—the defender steals the ball. Then I explained the real *why*: "Your mother and grandmother will be horrified if you have the ball stolen in front of the entire crowd." From that point forward, they began dribbling the basketball properly with their proper hand. Knowing the *why* brings confidence to stick with your decisions.

The *why* also drives open and up-front communication, which is crucial to the advisor-client relationship. As I've said before, when you understand why recommendations are made and what problems they hope to solve, you are far more apt to stick with them long-term. Given the explanation for why something is done a certain way, you'll realize that the advisor has listened to your goals and is looking out for your best interests. Many people say, "That makes sense." That builds more confidence for your planning, and increased confidence results in better decisions—decisions that may determine the difference between mediocrity and success.

Even though you may know your *why*, it can get buried under legalese and jargon. Without the right caddy, you could be left stranded in the rough, with the tourney on the line and the wrong club in your hand. Chapter 8 shows why it's so important to keep it simple and focused.

CHAPTER EIGHT

KEEP IT SIMPLE
BUT FOCUSED

That's been one of my mantras—focus and simplicity. Simple can be harder than complex: You have to work hard to get your thinking clean to make it simple. But it's worth it in the end because once you get there, you can move mountains.

—STEVE JOBS

Business owners with $2 million to $10 million are increasingly looking to wealth management advisors to navigate the complexities of their long-term financial planning. They want to devote attention to growing their business while delegating their wealth management. With today's time constraints and the pace of change, you need to be efficient in all aspects of your life and business. Keeping things simple is an important component.

SIMPLE CLARIFIES FOCUS

One of the first questions I ask at client meetings is, "Has anything changed with you or your family that impacts your finances?"

Most often, they say no because I see them regularly. Sometimes, however, there are major changes. For instance, one client, the matriarch of a very close-knit family, told me, "Yes, my son is getting divorced."

I quickly grabbed the family's estate-planning folder, looked at their plan, and said, "Not good." Their estate plan needed a fairly drastic overhaul. If their son predeceased her or her husband, their soon-to-be ex-daughter-in-law would inherit a portion of their estate. That was obviously no longer a goal, which was a natural response and required immediate attention.

We set up a meeting with their attorney. In a couple of weeks, their plan was modified to account for their life change. At the end of the meeting with the attorney, the son was still getting divorced, but the family's plans were already in order. We kept it simple and asked one basic question about recent changes, and because of that we were able to avoid a situation that could have had a tremendous impact on their financial picture. Again, the right question was the catalyst.

REMEMBER TO KISS

When planning, always remind yourself of the KISS principle—Keep It Simple, Stupid. It's an effective way to grasp all the complexity in today's world.

What if you're married to a nonfinancial spouse? Can your spouse step in and manage your business? How about your personal finances? Have you ever explained to them what you do? Do they even know where your assets are located? You need to simplify the jargon, don't you?

I was meeting with a business owner client and his spouse (a retired registered nurse) about what to consider when his multi-million-dollar business sold. As we were talking matter-of-factly about their estate planning, she stopped me and asked, "What's a trust?" She had no experience making decisions about this much money; she just wanted their wealth protected. We stepped back and talked, in very simplistic terms, about what a trust is and why it might be part of their planning. She was relieved and far more capable of making decisions understanding her planning options.

Leonardo da Vinci said, "Simplicity is the ultimate sophistication." Communicating in plain English terms is an art. Some of the highest-paid speakers are those who can communicate very complicated topics to the masses in a way that makes sense. It seems to have worked for Jerry Seinfeld, hasn't it?

COST AND VALUE

A frequent objection to hiring a financial advisor is cost. As noted earlier, cost is only ever an issue in the absence of value. If you're still reading, value is clearly important to you. If you are working with an advisor, are you able to pick up the phone and get the answers you need? Does your advisor handle only your investment planning? Do you receive more comprehensive advice and relationship management with your other professional advisors? It's important to consider whether you have the right person doing your planning.

You probably have someone on staff you consider your "best" employee, and he or she is also likely your highest-paid employee. If you could duplicate this person, would you? Shouldn't you think along those same lines when hiring your other advisors? Having the right team is critical to your success. The quest for multigenerational wealth requires you to make hard decisions, just as you do for your business. If you truly want to get there, align yourself with people who will help you get to the next level. If you aren't receiving the advice you need, you may have to make the difficult decision to find someone who can provide it. Multigenerational wealth requires a lifetime of discipline and making good decisions.

Starting with your wealth manager, your professional advisors' most important task is to organize your planning in simple terms. The better they understand your unique set of circumstances, the better they can counsel you on wealth management tasks, so vital to you and your family. You then have the freedom and confidence to care for the goose so it can continue laying golden eggs.

CONCLUSION

People don't always make the right decisions, but the people that are still there even after you make the wrong decisions, are the ones you should never let go of.

—LOGAN ZANE HESSEFORT

Perhaps you view wealth differently when you come from a hardworking family from very humble beginnings, as I did. Few are fortunate enough to witness firsthand the dedication, sacrifice, and smart decision making necessary to pursue multigenerational wealth. My parents taught us kids the value of saving, long-term investing, and making objective decisions that lead to success. My wisdom is a result of learning from a smart man and paying the price for my own subpar decisions. I've lived and learned every bit of advice you've read in this book, both from experiencing the challenges and understanding the hardships endured by several generations of my family.

Looking back, it's rewarding to see the positive results from executing on the fundamentals, hard work, and discipline. When you're born into a hypercompetitive family, you develop a passion for winning. It's what drives you. The relief on people's faces when they execute their estate-planning documents or save money on taxes is even *better*. We also see it on the face of a surviving spouse when they understand that they're still on track because of the planning that's been in place over the years. It is such a liberating feeling for clients, like a weight has been lifted and they can breathe easier. That sense of being on track, of having the financial wherewithal to maintain the lifestyle to which they've become accustomed, is irreplaceable.

People seem so much more relieved to have a plan and a caddy to help them navigate the course of life.

DELEGATE TO THE EXPERTS

Business owners often tell me that they don't trust themselves. They look in the mirror and say, "I understand I need to manage my money prudently, but I don't trust myself to do it right. What do I need to do to retire when I want while avoiding major financial mistakes?"

Repeatedly, I hear this level of fear, of people worrying they'll make the wrong decisions at the wrong time. Little mistakes can fester over the years, resulting in big problems later. This self-distrust leads them to say, "I need help."

The husband of one of our clients once came to me and said, "I tried to manage my money myself. I lost nearly all my money, hundreds of thousands of dollars, trading internet stocks, and I had to file for bankruptcy." It was a situation I didn't know anything about until after it was too late. At that point, there wasn't an advisor alive who could help him. The money was gone and he and his wife's lives were forever changed. I wonder, if he could go back in time and pay an advisor, would he? Almost certainly.

I see more and more people recognizing the need to delegate their most personal financial goals to a caddy who watches over their future and their family...it's just too complicated. More than just a business relationship, they want a long-term relationship with someone who knows and appreciates their goals. When people become clients of our firm, they become more than just "customers"; they become like family.

DON'T FORGET THE SIX CS

In order to create goals, design the playbook of what you want your financial future to look like. Then each and every financial decision works toward the same purpose: multigenerational wealth. Proper planning lessens the probability of errors, leading to fewer surprises down the road. Minimizing major mistakes is a prerequisite for maintaining long-term wealth. Having a coach who embodies the Six Cs most important to you—Character, Chemistry, Caring, Competence, Cost Effectiveness, and Consultative—is a prudent start to increasing the probability of your family's financial success.

Find the right advisor to guide your family's multigenerational planning. Share your life's story with them; not just your successes, but even more importantly, your failures. Impart your values so that they can provide you with a highly personalized and customized plan—one with a laser focus on what you want to accomplish. Then move forward into your most successful life, feeling confident about your future.

THE SIMPLEST FIX

Many years ago, I was talking to a business owner about his personal life. His goose laid quite large golden eggs—and a lot of them. The problem, however, was that his work-life balance was tipped heavily toward work. Managing his business and employees was taking a toll on him. The problem was simple to fix, but he couldn't see it. He needed to let go of what he didn't need to do at work. I recommended what our business caddies tell us: "Do the three things you do best and hire someone else to do everything else. If someone can do it 75 percent as well as you can, have them do it." This gentleman did just that, and his business quickly trended upward. The simple act of empowering the right people to help him with the day-to-day operations allowed him to take better care of the goose, make more money, and improve his quality of life.

When faced with the possibility of problems, there are two possible responses: you can bury your head in the sand and do nothing, or you can get help. Would you and your family be better served hiring the right professionals to provide sound ongoing advice? Most business owners feel a sense of relief when they understand their family can rely on someone to guide them through good times and bad. They just want to take care of the goose and enjoy time with their family.

Many business owners comment on how refreshing it is when they make the move to work with a wealth manager. They know someone understands what they want to accomplish and is watching over their financial affairs. Outsourcing their personal affairs to professionals allows them to focus on taking care of the goose—making sure she continues laying the eggs their family relies on for security.

I'M HERE TO HELP

If you think you'd like to interview a financial caddy to explore how wealth management can benefit you and your family, I'd love to hear from you. It's easy to reach me on my website at www.Marrella.com, by telephone at (610) 655-9700, or via email at paul.marrella@raymondjames.com. Let's discuss what you are trying to accomplish to determine whether a Stress-Test or Discovery Meeting may be helpful for you.

ACKNOWLEDGMENTS

I'm a guy who never passed a grammar test in high school and yet is now a second-time author. As such, it seems easier to name those I *don't* have to thank (they number very few).

From my parents, to my teachers, to my coaches, to my mentors, wife, and friends—you all had a part in this. Without your constant "constructive criticism," I never would have made it through junior high, let alone authorship.

To all of you, thanks!

ABOUT THE AUTHOR

Paul started his advisor career while he was a law student. After a brief but rewarding legal career, he followed a childhood dream as an equity trader on Wall Street. A half decade later, he joined his father to reinvent the family business. He's currently an owner/managing partner of his family business, a licensed attorney, CERTIFIED FINANCIAL PLANNER™ Professional, and Retirement Income Certified Professional (RICP). His diverse and unique background has provided him with perspectives on the world that add value to his clients by addressing problems from various angles. He works with down-to-earth, millionaire-next-door types who have strong family values. And sometimes their business is their family. Paul is highly competitive and has learned key lessons from sports, especially that hard work and discipline beat talent almost every time.

He is married with two kids, and is a big sports fan.

DISCLAIMER

Certified Financial Planner Board of Standards Inc. owns the certification marks CFP®, CERTIFIED FINANCIAL PLANNER™, CFP® (with plaque design), and CFP® (with flame design) in the US, which it awards to individuals who successfully complete CFP Board's initial and ongoing certification requirements.

The information contained in this book does not purport to be a complete description of the securities, markets, or developments referred to in this material. The information has been obtained from sources considered to be reliable, but we do not guarantee that the foregoing material is accurate or complete. Any information is not a complete summary or statement of all available data necessary for making an investment decision and does

Securities offered through Raymond James Financial Services, Inc. Member FINRA/SIPC. Investment advisory services are offered through Raymond James Financial Services Advisors, Inc. Marrella Financial Group, LLC is not a registered broker/dealer and is independent of Raymond James Financial Services.